HAY HOUSE BASICS

GODDESS
WISDOM

GODDESS WISDOM

Connect to the Power of the
Sacred Feminine through
Ancient Teachings and Practices

TANISHKA

HAY
HOUSE

HAY HOUSE

Carlsbad, California • New York City • London
Sydney •Johannesburg • Vancouver • New Delhi

First published and distributed in the United Kingdom by:
Hay House UK Ltd, Astley House, 33 Notting Hill Gate, London W11 3JQ
Tel: +44 (0)20 3675 2450; Fax: +44 (0)20 3675 2451; www.hayhouse.co.uk

Published and distributed in the United States of America by:
Hay House Inc., PO Box 5100, Carlsbad, CA 92018-5100
Tel: (1) 760 431 7695 or (800) 654 5126; Fax: (1) 760 431 6948 or (800) 650 5115
www.hayhouse.com

Published and distributed in Australia by:
Hay House Australia Ltd, 18/36 Ralph St, Alexandria NSW 2015
Tel: (61) 2 9669 4299; Fax: (61) 2 9669 4144; www.hayhouse.com.au

Published and distributed in the Republic of South Africa by:
Hay House SA (Pty) Ltd, PO Box 990, Witkoppen 2068
info@hayhouse.co.za; www.hayhouse.co.za

Published and distributed in India by:
Hay House Publishers India, Muskaan Complex, Plot No.3, B-2,
Vasant Kunj, New Delhi 110 070
Tel: (91) 11 4176 1620; Fax: (91) 11 4176 1630; www.hayhouse.co.in

Distributed in Canada by:
Raincoast Books, 2440 Viking Way, Richmond, B.C. V6V 1N2
Tel: (1) 604 448 7100; Fax: (1) 604 270 7161; www.raincoast.com

A catalogue record for this book is available from the British Library.

ISBN: 978-1-78180-903-7

Interior illustrations: 80 Belynda Simpson; 97, 125 Carmen Payne; 193t
Chudomir Tsankov; 193b Patrick Guenette; 194t sputanski; 194b yod
pimsen; 195t Denis Barbulat; 195m original drawing by Jeff Saward,
final graphic by Vicki Keiser; 195b colorvalley; 196t mtmmarek; 196b
Nadejda Tchijova; 197t Mila Gligoric; 197b Vadym Malyshevskyi;
198t ARCHITECTEUR; 198b stefanina hill; 199 redlinevector

Printed in the UK by TJ International Ltd, Padstow, Cornwall.

To those of you who commit to make the journey to the landscape within – may your path be blessed with the light of truth.

Contents

List of exercises

Introduction

My journey with the Goddess

Have you ever wondered why the creator God is said to be male, although it's women who give birth? Perhaps you've questioned the fact that in school, we learn more about the deeds of men than those of women? Or thought, 'What does it mean to be a woman – beyond looking sexy and being kind?'

If you have an intuitive feeling that there's secret wisdom that you've been denied – holding the key to empowering your feminine sense of self – this book is for you. It's your yearning and your curiosity that initiated this meeting, so it's my pleasure to share with you your ancient birthright of sacred feminine wisdom.

As your guide on this adventure, I feel I should explain what makes me an expert on the subject. So, here's my story. (You may recognize parts of your own story.)

Girl least likely to be nominated a Goddess

I never thought this is what I'd end up doing with my life. Empowering women to live like Goddesses was certainly not an option offered by the careers guidance counselor at my high school. No, my journey with the Goddess began when I got lost...

I was 26 and a walking pin-up girl for dysfunction. My primary relationships were with my cat and my gay best friend – with whom I was hopelessly infatuated, so there was no happy ending at the end of *that* rainbow! The way I made my living was also far from fulfilling: I was working alternate nights as a stand-up comedienne and a stripper (occupations that seemed compatible, somehow, at the time).

So, when I wasn't taking my clothes off for money, I'd paint myself up, unleash my big hair like a fearful animal attempting to look imposing, and then strut on stage wearing my Glamazon armor, fueled with a caffeinated energy drink. I'd then attempt to make drunk men laugh by putting myself down. I don't recommend that as a self-esteem-building exercise.

On other evenings, I'd be draped around a pole, trying to feel more like Gypsy Rose Lee than a zoo exhibit, as I seduced men into helping me pay the rent on my overpriced inner-city apartment. Working in such demeaning environments meant a large proportion of my income was spent self-soothing with a toxic array of pot, cigarettes, chocolate, caffeine, and alcohol.

One night, eclipsed by emotional overwhelm, I got down on my knees and said to the Universe: 'If you want me to be a woman, then send me some f**king role models!' That's when it happened. The Goddess answered my call, and like magic, the life I'd known was swept away. I soon found myself in a forest, being initiated into a circle of women at my first Goddess workshop.

My early life as a tomboy

Growing up, no one ever told me I was a Goddess, or that I could aspire to be one. My father's nicknames for me were 'scruff bucket' and 'dog's breakfast,' on account of my wild child appearance. Unlike my sister, who always managed to keep her clothes (and her dolls) neat, clean, and orderly, I'd usually have my undergarments protruding and dirt under my fingernails. My dolls' hair was matted and defied taming – a reflection of my own afro curls.

As the second-born daughter I quickly recognized that my older sister had already fulfilled the role of 'Daddy's girl,' so at a young age I gave up on the idea of trying to steal her title. I didn't fit the image of the feminine ideal – a good girl with straight blonde hair who was quiet and clean – so I rebelled by no longer trying to be feminine.

Instead, I sought attention by being funny and clever. When approval for that wasn't forthcoming, my inner achiever went into overdrive. I started collecting 'A' grades, trophies, certificates, and praise from my teachers.

The more I operated out of the masculine part of my psyche, taking action to win approval, the more people related to me as a tomboy, and the more masculine I became. Although I enjoyed dancing as a hobby, I was usually cast as a 'boy' in the annual ballet school concert, on account of being 'tall.' While I complied, I felt humiliated that I wasn't seen as making the cut as a girl.

Puberty without initiation into womanhood

Growing up in the 'ballet world,' the development of hips and breasts were unwelcome guests, as any sign of fertility undermined the balletic feminine ideal of an ethereal waif. So while one might think this was an environment that nurtured feminine traits such as grace and poise, there was a misogynistic undertone. Fortunately for me, unlike my sister, I didn't have the talent or the physique to become a professional dancer, so I was spared daily weighing sessions and calorie counting.

However, I was keen to pursue a life on the stage in musical theater, so I still experienced pressure to be thin and attractive. This was reinforced by a fridge magnet bought by my mother, which declared: 'Thin is in.' In hindsight, I think it's a small miracle that neither I nor my sister developed an eating disorder.

As for learning about sex, I have a vague memory of reading a book about female puberty called *What's Happening to Me?* But most of what I learned at a young age came from lunchtime conversations with the other girls at primary school. This included a great deal of misinformation that was later clarified by reading the 'Dolly Doctor' column in *Dolly* magazine when I started high school.

The one 'sex education' class at school was a science lesson that included diagrams of fallopian tubes – this was derailed when everyone started laughing at a more sheltered classmate who thought that female genitals were called 'Virginia.'

When I officially 'became a woman' with the arrival of my first period, I'd had no prior conversations with my mother that had left the door open for me to speak with her about it. So I hid the evidence of my period like a criminal, until I could get my head around what had happened.

Meanwhile at school, I was being voted 'the ugliest girl in the class' by a ballot paper passed around every Friday during our music lesson. This humiliation was the result of my mother not letting me shave my legs. To recover, I'd shut myself in our bathroom after school and give myself a private makeover – like a closet cross-dresser – to prove how seductive I could be.

This involved using my stage make-up to paint myself up like Joan Collins – the reigning soap star of the 1980s – followed by a dance routine to a Shirley Bassey song in the living room. That would abruptly come to an end when I heard Mum's car pull into the driveway...it's fair to say, I felt more like a drag queen than a teenage girl.

Looking for love in all the wrong places

Like many young women growing up in a patriarchal culture, I based my worth on that which I observed women were primarily valued for – sexual attractiveness. So in my late teens and early twenties I searched for love through attempts to enchant men with my attractiveness. The result was heartbreak, STDs, and sexual abuse.

This is a story I've heard echoed by countless women in my workshops over the past 20 years. It's a taboo side of maidenhood that results in deep levels of shame. This pattern is amplified if a young woman's father has no understanding or respect for feminine values. His cultural dismissal is taken as a personal rejection by his daughter, resulting in her choosing partners (male or female) who only value what women can do for them as lovers or mothers. And serial seduction driven by low self-esteem is not a recipe for self-fulfillment.

Synchronicity, magic, and miracles

About a year before that fateful day when I called out to the Universe for some role models, I took a job in a pizza restaurant. Two of the delivery guys there, who were Polish, addressed me as 'Tanishka': a pet name for 'Tania,' my birth name. It resonated through me like a gong of truth, emanating my core essence. Years later, I discovered Tanishka is an ancient Sanskrit name meaning 'Goddess of Gold.'

The turning point came shortly after, when I met a couple of women who'd volunteered to crew the cabaret show I was performing with my drag queen friends. Taking pity on my apparent lack of feminine empowerment, they invited me to stay at their farm and accompany them to a weekend Goddess workshop being run by Jen Powell in Australia's Otway Ranges.

Wrapped in blankets and armed with art supplies and journals, we sat in a circle on a beautiful mountain property, listening attentively to the pearls of wisdom flowing from this gently spoken, wise woman. I was the youngest one there, and for the first time in my life I witnessed the power of feminine insight. This ignited a burning desire for more!

After that experience I didn't want to return to my miserable life in the city, which felt void of meaning, so the women of the forest helped me to find a small cottage I could afford. Situated at the end of Seven Bridges Road, it was a symbolic herald of my inner journey to unveil my seven feminine archetypes. Beneath the cottage was an underground lake, making it a receptive portal for intuitive information downloads.

And, as the location was off the grid, I spent my 10-month sabbatical there unplugged from all media. That meant no electro-magnetic pollution could interfere with the reception of my subtle senses. I spent my days doing whatever my intuition directed me to do – such as self-initiation rituals, yoga, meditation, art therapy, channeled writing, and dream analysis. I also read a room full of books on ancient women's wisdom, myth symbolism, faerytales, mysticism, and the esoteric traditions.

Jen Powell became my faery godmother. I would visit her to borrow books and to ask for guidance on everything from my own process to the research materials I was devouring. Whenever I stayed at Jen's home, I slept in a bed beneath a giant painting she'd created of the Cretan snake Goddess, who I suspect shared information with me in my dreaming state.

At the end of my sabbatical I was guided to run a weekend Goddess workshop. The experience was so uplifting, and I knew I'd found my calling. I dedicated myself to serving the Goddess – using my priestess name, Tanishka – and have spent the past two decades disseminating ancient feminine wisdom and practices.

Getting the most out of this book

Whether you're just opening the door to the Goddess or have been walking the path for many years, I've created this book with you in mind.

Goddess gifts of present, past, and future

In Part 1, we begin the journey with a look at why the Goddess is rising again after thousands of years of obscurity. You'll need to put on some comfortable shoes as we dig around the rubble of ancient Goddess sites to discover where and how the sacred feminine was once celebrated, and why the Goddess disappeared.

I then demystify the evil enchantment cast over all things feminine, and review the damage caused by the suppression of worship of the divine in a feminine form. Finally, you'll learn all the ways that Goddess traditions keep women sane in a world gone mad; and how to stop giving yourself a hard time about not being someone else's idea of 'the perfect woman.'

Secret women's business

Part 2 dives into the most important information any woman could hope to have – the ancient teachings that were once every woman's birthright. Here, among other things, you will learn to:

1. Reduce your daily stress levels and have more energy.

2. Get more support (and reduce comfort eating).

3. Stop comparing yourself with other women and silence your inner critic.

4. Transcend the fear of aging, and love getter older.

5. Value yourself in all your choices and feel empowered as a woman.

6. Befriend your period and understand the effect of the lunar cycle on your moods.

7. Enhance your intuition and grow your wisdom.

8. Feel juicy and alive with Goddess mojo!

Exercises

To help you unleash your inner Goddess, I've included empowering activities and exercises throughout the book. I encourage you to take a few moments to complete these en route, as they'll create shifts within your psyche and help you anchor the lessons contained within each chapter. By the end of this experiential journey, you'll emanate divine radiance!

Yin is in

Finally, at the end of each chapter I've included suggestions for what I've called 'Yin reflection time.' The feminine way of learning is more intuitive than rational – the way we're taught in school – so to encourage you to attune to your intuition (inner knowing), I invite you to pause at the end of each chapter and reflect on what you've read.

This will create the space to access your own insights, and any relevant memories that are evoked by the connections you make while reading each chapter. This approach will help you to gain much more from this book.

Part I

FOUNDATIONS

Chapter 1
The return of the sacred feminine

There's evidence everywhere demonstrating the return of the Goddess and the sacred feminine. However, there are misconceptions about what exactly the *Goddess* and the *sacred feminine* are, so before we venture further, let's define them.

Introducing the Goddess/sacred feminine

A Goddess is a divine being embodied in a feminine form. She's one who is revered for possessing supernatural powers. Ancient peoples around the world once worshipped the Goddess in her many forms – from the brave huntress to the erotic lover.

However, her most central role was the primordial creatrix (supreme feminine creator). This deep honoring of the Mother Goddess was based on the early communities' direct, intimate, and symbiotic relationship with the Earth.

Early peoples were mystics who studied the patterns and movements of the stars in order to chart weather patterns, determine hunting seasons, and navigate by both land and sea. In contrast to our modern tendency to fear both the dark and the unknown, our ancestors worshipped the cosmic void – the place of pure potential from which all life emerges as the holy feminine principle.

The term sacred feminine simply refers to the conscious expression of all feminine traits, qualities, and values that are essential to the whole, and are therefore holy. Ancient Goddess teachings and traditions focused on self-knowledge through the getting of wisdom. Wisdom teachings were highly prized, and ritualistic customs developed to help people grow their wisdom.

Contrary to our modern misconception, a Goddess is *not* a woman who possesses more sex appeal than mere mortal women. This idea was perpetuated by the early Hollywood film industry, which portrayed some of its female stars as 'Goddesses' – leading them to be worshipped as muses. The resulting legacy left many women feeling less than divine by comparison.

The Goddess is making a comeback

The truth is, every woman is a Goddess – once she understands that she's inherently divine by design.

When we make this shift within our psyche, we start honoring ourselves accordingly – in our choices. This is the phenomenon currently taking place globally. It's changing the cultural landscape, and creating a legacy for our daughters. It's an exciting time to be here in a female body!

We're now emerging from approximately 5,000 years of patriarchal conditioning: a mindset and culture which taught that the divine had an exclusively male expression, while simultaneously casting the feminine as an evil temptress who ought not to be trusted. This perspective impacted all layers of human experience, and resulted in women being valued primarily for their attractiveness to men and their ability to bear sons.

The patriarchal mindset also resulted in women becoming marginalized, and prevented from holding positions of external power. In the 20th century, the two world wars ushered in widespread social change that granted women more freedom; however, even today, the halls of power are still off limits to many women – unless they are willing to check their feminine sensibilities at the door and adopt a masculine approach when seeking access to the elite's old boys' club.

So, to better understand why there's a growing interest in the Goddess and the sacred feminine today, let's gain a broader perspective on it.

The astrological ages

The feminine way of recording time and interpreting social and cultural events is to chart the cycles of nature and their influence. This is a very different approach from the masculine concept of 'history,' which is a linear account focusing largely on the documentation of 'great' battles and empires, seen from the perspective of the victor. To understand the difference between these two methods of charting time, let's look at the celestial cycles that have shaped humanity.

In Western astrology, the 12 'astrological ages' are celestial cycles of time lasting approximately 2,000 years (the average time it takes for the vernal equinox to move from one constellation of the zodiac into the next).[1] Astrologers have observed that the astrological ages affect life here on Earth by influencing the rise and fall of civilizations, and cultural, social, and political developments.

Below is a brief overview of the last six astrological ages that illustrates the rise and fall of the Goddess. It's followed by a description of the age we're entering now – the Age of Aquarius – which is ushering in the *return* of the Goddess.

Note: Unlike our annual solar and monthly lunar transits around the 12 signs of the zodiac, the astrological ages cycle in reverse. The dates shown below are estimates, due to the 'cusp' period between each age when new influences gradually reach a tipping point and collapse the old paradigm.

Age of Leo: 10,000–8000BCE

Leo is a Fire sign ruled by the Sun, so it's not surprising that during the Mesolithic era (between the Paleolithic and Neolithic eras), the glaciers that had covered most of the Northern hemisphere melted. This caused the sea level to rise by 90m (300 ft)[2]; in turn, this warmed the climate and fertility returned to the Earth. (Some continents, such as Australia, saw sea levels rise in the previous age, around 12,000BCE.)

Animal and plant species increased, which supported population growth. Understandably, people worshipped the Sun. Archaeologists have found accounts of Sun Goddesses in Canaan (Palestine), Anatolia (Turkey), Arabia, and Australia, and also among the Inuit, the Japanese, and the Khasis of India.[3]

While there is archaeological evidence of Goddess worship from as early as 30,000BCE, the rise in population during the Age of Leo saw the Goddess teachings and stories that had been kept alive during the ice age – via stone carvings and the oral tradition of storytelling – disseminated more widely.

Age of Cancer: 8000–6000BCE

Cancer is a Water sign that's governed by the Moon. It teaches us how to grow with the natural cycles and find strength in the shared resources of community. So this period – the Neolithic, or New Stone Age – saw matriarchal Goddess-worshipping settlements develop and flourish in the lush fertile delta regions of Mesopotamia (a region roughly corresponding to the modern Middle East) and Eastern Europe and in the wet climate areas of Asia and South America.

There was a widespread shift from nomadic lifestyles to settled agricultural communities, which resulted in more population growth. Central to daily life were baking rites in accordance with the lunar cycles, and women's lunar blood was revered and used to consecrate sacred amulets, temples, and graves.

Archaeologists have discovered and documented Goddess relics from female-centric communities of this era who honored the Mother Goddess and lived without war for thousands of years.

Age of Gemini: 6000–4000BCE

Gemini is the mercurial Air sign of ideas, communication, and commerce, and during this period, people ventured far beyond their settlements. They exchanged ideas, and domestic crafts and techniques that had been developed and refined during the Age of Cancer.

The Earth-based Goddess traditions that had dominated societies before the advent of recorded history developed into more complex and organized religious structures during this period. The evidence for this is seen in the Goddess artifacts found throughout Mesopotamia and 'Old Europe' – a term coined by archaeologist Marija Gimbutas to describe what she saw as a relatively homogeneous pre-Indo-European Neolithic culture in southeastern Europe.[4,5]

The Age of Gemini coincided with the emergence of the proto-Indo-European language around 5000BCE: the parent language of many of those spoken today.[6] It's also when symbolism began to appear in art. Culture was prized as a sign of a civilized society, so priests and priestesses enjoyed high status as the keepers of culture; they ensured all forms of sacred art were preserved.

Age of Taurus: 4000–2000BCE

Taurus is an Earth sign ruled by Venus, the feminine planet of beauty, love, and sensual pleasure. This influence inspired works of art and architecture. Since Taurus is also the sign of the master builder who values physical possessions, this era had a distinct focus on generating material resources and wealth. As a result, the temples became the money-lenders, with 'good fortune' interpreted as tangible proof they had won favor with the gods.

Ziggurats and pyramids were erected, underpinned by sacred geometry. These were used to house sacred rites designed to create Heaven on Earth by embodying the divine in human form, and marrying both divine feminine and masculine principles.

The Goddess was celebrated throughout the world during this era, with established temples dedicated to numerous aspects of her offering guidance, healing, prayer, esoteric study, and initiation rites to nurture the soul development of both men and women.

Age of Aries: 2000BCE–1CE

Aries is a Fire sign and the first zodiac sign. It evokes the child who seeks individuation from the mother by embarking on a quest to prove his or her courage and attain glory as a hero. This was the era when the patriarchy sought to overthrow the matriarchy, with the rise of empires and dynasties that demanded duty to the state over the feminine values that had previously been considered sacred.

Ares was the ancient Greek God of War, so this era was bloodthirsty. Brutal forces desecrated Earth-worshipping agricultural settlements to assert their dominance over the land and people. This is when the Old Testament of the Bible was written to document the history of a dynastic line of patriarchs who led their people out of slavery to serve a vengeful father God who punished those who didn't follow his word.

It's also when the patriarchal creation myth of the War God Marduk emerged in Babylon in Mesopotamia[7]; Marduk is credited with destroying the Mother Goddess, Tiamat, who was cast as evil.[8] The high-ranking temple priestesses who served the Goddess were reduced to tokenistic ceremonial roles for public show, and schools were created in Mesopotamia that only educated boys.[9]

Essentially, this era is when the Earth Goddess of Love (Taurus), who was previously worshipped with creative sacred sexual rites, was overthrown by the Fire God of War (Ares), whose God demanded allegiance, with the threat of destruction.

Age of Pisces: 1–2000CE

Pisces is the element of Water and the last sign in the zodiac. Pisces asks us to reflect on our actions to become wise, instead of blaming, which creates conflict. Pisces evokes the inner mystic – symbolized by the two fish that swim in opposite directions: one to the light and the other to the watery depths of the subconscious. This is the sign of the resurrected world savior who ends conflict through empathetic understanding.

Pisces is ruled by Neptune, the planet of sleep, dreams, and illusions. In this era, the spiritual dogma institutionalized by reigning empires was used to deceive people into a sleep state of docile obedience, resulting in widespread delusion. Scriptures taught that Heaven and Earth were separate entities: Heaven was associated with the masculine and the Earth was associated with the feminine. Transcendence was sought through a mental ideal of purity: the sensual realm was denied, and demonized as impure.

A suppression of the natural laws taught in the earlier Goddess tradition ushered in an unprecedented mass global destruction of natural resources.

Age of Aquarius: 2000–4000ce

Aquarius is an Air sign ruled by Uranus, which evokes a spirit of unity and oneness. This influence translates into unconventional innovations, and humanitarian ideals that serve the greater good. With the emergence of the internet, we've already witnessed mass communication transmitted through the airwaves. This supports free speech, enables the sharing of ideas and information, and promotes a global outlook that catalyzes positive social change.

Hierarchical power structures are falling – replaced by unilateral workplaces and online niche micro-businesses. Technological advances, combined with growing public awareness, will ensure power that has been withheld will be shared as a universal human right. And instead of seeing divinity as something external, more of us are becoming aware of the eternal consciousness within, and awakening our consciousness by practicing energy raising, healing, and manifestation techniques.

A signal of the Goddess's return

The growing influence of the Age of Aquarius is ending the perception of duality as a fixed reality. So, rather than seeing everything in rational 'black and white' terms, we're perceiving more through our subtle senses – governed by the feminine part of our psyche. This growing appreciation of feminine traits such as empathy and intuition is deconstructing traditional gender roles, as both men and women seek to strengthen their feminine side.

We're also seeing the rise of women as leaders of social change, alongside men who have developed their feminine traits. This has led to the creation of charitable programs that support victims of the old patriarchy: among these are orphanages, schools, medical programs, and rehabilitation programs for survivors of the sex-trafficking industry. There are also lobby groups demanding legislation to curb industries that endanger public health and employ ecological destruction for their own profit and power.

Social media is also giving women a public voice and a place to gather; it's galvanizing the power of sisterhood as a force for positive global change. This is bringing about the dissemination of ancient women's wisdom and sacred traditions. Through the power of community, women are supporting each other to heal and grow.

Women, and men, are increasingly taking up Eastern practices such as yoga and meditation to counteract unsustainable levels of stress, and urbanites are seeking a greater connection with Mother Nature through natural therapies, remedies, and relocation to rural areas.

The 'third wave' of the women's movement

This reclamation of ancient feminine wisdom and sacred customs marks the 'third wave' of feminine emancipation worldwide. So, upon the shoulders of giants we stand and offer our gratitude to:

❖ **Women's suffrage campaigners.** In the mid-19th century, women in several countries formed organizations to fight for women's right to vote and stand for political office, starting the first wave of the women's movement. The first country to grant national-level voting rights to women was New Zealand (1893), and by 1920, many nations had followed. In 2011, Saudi Arabia became the latest state to grant women the right to vote; this became effective in the 2015 municipal elections.

❖ **The Women's Liberation Movement.** This 'second wave' of feminism grew out of the civil rights movement in the late sixties and early seventies, and fought for the reproductive, legal, and economic equality of women. This coincided with feminist academics revealing evidence of ancient Goddess-worshipping cultures.

If you're interested in learning more about the history of the women's movement, I'd recommend watching these films: *You're Beautiful When You're Angry*, 2014 (US documentary); *Suffragette*, 2015 (UK drama); *Iron Jawed Angels*, 2004 (US drama).

Rise of the Amazons!

Those born during the peak of the Women's Liberation Movement are now in their mid-life phase, which is their second maidenhood. This is when their inner warrioress is evoked and they discover their strength in sisterhood. So the daughters of the feminists are at the forefront of this third wave.

Reclaiming our culture

We could identify the current wave of uppity women as the 'Goddesses or priestesses.' These are the women who are seeking spiritual equality through the recovery and dissemination of Goddess cultural traditions and spiritual teachings – on the understanding that this empowers feminine values in the wider community. By reclaiming feminine spirituality, women are reconnecting with their inner power, making this a spiritual movement rather than a political one.

This approach differs from the first two waves of the women's movement in that it accesses and promotes the feminine gifts most vehemently denied by the patriarchy – our intuitive, psychic, and healing abilities. It also reclaims our sacred traditions, which are the ultimate taboos of feminine expression within a patriarchal culture.

Despite the growing number of women discovering Goddess teachings and traditions, in academia the Goddess tradition is still often undermined through a language bias. In his book *Genesis of the Grail Kings*, author Laurence Gardner observes, 'Because of the sexist conditioning of male-dominated society, the harmonious male-and-female spirit of all early tradition has been lost, so that veneration of the male deity is now called "religion", whereas veneration of any feminine aspect is called a "cult".'[10]

The Bible also undermines the sacred feminine in numerous ways, including referring to the celestial Mother Goddess as 'The Great Whore of Babylon.' Jonathan Kirsch, author of *Harlot by the Side of the Road: Forbidden Tales of the Bible*, suggests that the Hebrew Bible (from *biblion*, meaning 'papyrus') was pieced together from various sources and developed over the span of several centuries.[11]

> **Even religion gets recycled!**
>
> The authors of the Hebrew Bible reused stories from sacred feminine traditions. For example, the hymns to the Babylonian Goddess Ishtar from the *Hieros Gamos* (sacred marriage) rite appear at the end of the Old Testament as the Song of Songs.[12]
>
> The Old Testament story of Noah was appropriated from Sumerian tablets that spoke of the God Enki warning the Sumerian king Ziusudra to build an ark in anticipation of a great flood. The story of Moses was based on that of Sargon of Akkad, who was sent upstream in a basket as a baby, but was rescued and went on to become ruler of the Akkadian empire in Mesopotamia.[13] The story of Moses parting the Red Sea was taken from the ancient Egyptian story of the Goddess Isis parting the seas.[14]

Becoming part of the rising feminine

When women realize that the patriarchy has desecrated, repressed, and misrepresented the sacred feminine, it's understandable that we may feel a sense of injustice. However, nothing is gained by perpetuating a mindset of 'us and them,' as this only creates inner and outer conflict.

It's futile to expend energy on righteous anger that seeks to blame rather than resolve this cultural imbalance between the portrayal of the sacred feminine and masculine. Given the widespread societal breakdown and ecological disaster it has caused, we need to focus instead on creative solutions.

The only way forward is to recognize that our core spiritual beliefs directly influence the status and expression of gender polarities in society. This goes beyond a 'war of the sexes,' because expression of the feminine has also been denied in men. This is why laws and initiatives introduced to impose physical gender equality – without addressing the underlying *belief* system – will only have a surface effect. Without healing our perception of the feminine as *equally* sacred and valuable in both men *and* women, we'll see an escalation of the following global trends, in which the feminine is being sold, desecrated, and consumed:

❖ Sex trafficking of minors and women.

❖ Widespread pedophilia, both privately and in organized pedophilia rings.

❖ Ritual abuse performed on minors and women in secret societies and religious cults.

❖ Sexualization of toys and clothes aimed at young girls.

❖ Online predators targeting teenagers via social media.

❖ The online mail-order bride industry.

❖ College campus cultures that promote rape and demeaning initiation rites.

❖ Cyber bullying and sexting among teens.

❖ A global pandemic of pornography that perpetuates the degradation and disempowerment of the feminine.

❖ An increase in violent fetish imagery.

❖ Violent video games and toys marketed to underage boys.

❖ Rising rates of suicide among men, due to social expectations to suppress emotion.

❖ Violence against women, including sexual assault and domestic abuse.

❖ Female genital mutilation; executions and societal exclusion of women.

❖ Widespread cosmetic surgery and eating disorders.

❖ Increased infertility due to exposure to toxic chemicals.

❖ Contaminated food and water sources.

❖ Genetically modified food and unsustainable and inhumane farming methods.

Working together

Fortunately, the return of the sacred feminine is being championed by both men and women dedicated to restoring the sacred balance.

At the 2009 Vancouver Peace Summit in Canada, the Dalai Lama said: 'The world will be saved by the Western woman.'[15] He was implying that women in the developed nations have the freedom and the means to make a difference.

Perhaps more importantly, though, when we heal the feminine in ourselves – a process you will learn as you read this book – we create a ripple effect within our overtly masculine culture. The 16th-century physician and seer Nostradamus also predicted the fall of the patriarchy and the rise of the sacred feminine at this time in human evolution; he said: 'The great barbarian empire of men decay, Before the Moon completes its cycle.'

It starts with us

To heal the sacred balance, we all need to question whether our values, priorities, and beliefs are still underpinned by the patriarchal conditioning we received while growing up in a culture that denies, ridicules, and minimizes the sacred feminine.

Exercise: Acknowledging the inner patriarch

Complete this short quiz to determine the dominance of your 'inner patriarch.'

Question 1: You have a big decision to make. Do you:

A.   Seek advice from an authority figure.

B.   Analyze the pros and cons.

C.   Go with your intuition.

Question 2: Why did you choose your current career/job?

A.   To acquire success, recognition, and a great income.

B.   To ensure stability by doing what you're good at.

C.   To pursue personal fulfillment and make a difference.

Question 3: Which of the following best describes you?

A.   Very traditional.

B.   Somewhat conservative, but open to change.

C.   Counter-cultural.

Analysis time!

Mainly A: you value the external more than the internal, which suggests your inner patriarch is dominant. Mainly B: you try to take both external and internal factors into account; therefore, your inner patriarch is in transition. Mainly C: you've developed inner authority, so your inner patriarch is in the back seat.

Embodying the feminine can change the world

We're living in challenging times, but scientific developments have revealed that even our smallest actions *do* make a difference to the whole. In 1997, Argentine theoretical physicist Juan Maldacena proposed that the Universe is a holographic projection.[16] This idea was generally accepted as valid, but conclusive proof was not forthcoming. Then, in 2013, simulations conducted by Yoshifumi Hyakutake of Ibaraki University in Japan offered compelling evidence that Maldacena's theory was plausible.[17]

The concept that everything is a reflection in the interwoven web of life is nothing new. Indigenous people have accepted this as fact for thousands of years. Now, science also acknowledges that while we may not be able to specifically track the impact of a single small action on the macrocosm, that doesn't invalidate it. This concept is officially known as 'the chaos theory' but it was popularized as 'The Butterfly Effect.'[18]

What is chaos? It's the way of the feminine – a creative, spontaneous flow of life force that will completely transform us, if we embrace it with surrender and trust.

With this in mind, we can consider ourselves fractals of the Earth Mother: knowing that what we heal and empower in ourselves, we effect not only in the environment around us, but in the collective consciousness.

The alternative is to take a purely rational perspective, based on an analysis of the global crises we face today. On its own, this approach understandably induces overwhelm; however, if we combine our masculine ability to analyze with our feminine intuition, we will feel more empowered to make a difference – and our thought projections are perhaps the most significant element to affect the outcome.

Feminine ways to make a difference

So, it's important to access both our masculine and feminine attributes in order to effect positive global change. Most people are aware of the masculine approach – such as writing to our local representative in public office. But here's a list of simple actions to create positive social change that utilize our feminine strengths, such as healing, compassion, co-operation, and creative visualization. We can employ these whether we're male or female.

1. Be mindful of the power of our words to affect the future.

2. Utilize the power of community to create positive social change.

3. Heal the balance of feminine and masculine polarities within ourselves.

4. Heal the gender war externally by exercising brotherly/ sisterly love.

5. Seek to understand and empathize with those in other cultures.

6. Make choices that honor the sacredness of all life, to ensure sustainability.

Exercise: Goddess initiation rite

The following is an invitation to actively take part in this worldwide movement of social change – by adopting the mindset of one who sees and honors herself as a sacred vessel for the divine feminine.

You can complete this Goddess initiation rite on your own, or gather together a group of friends. The ideal time to perform it is Full Moon!

Make a Goddess crown

In preparation for this sacred rite, adorn your head with flowers as a daughter of Mother Earth. Gather some greenery (vines such as ivy are ideal) and flowers from your garden to make a crown. You may find it helpful to purchase floral wire beforehand, to make a frame that fits your head, and floral tape to bind any stems that are too short to wrap around the frame.

Enchant your creation

You will find many Goddess chants on You Tube that you can sing along to while crafting your Goddess crown. This ensures that what you're weaving is done with the loving intent of sisterhood.

Create a sacred space in a power place

Once adorned with your crown, head to a natural water source, such as a lake or river, or the ocean. If you can't get to a water source, collect some rainwater beforehand in a glass or a ceramic dish containing rose quartz and/or rose petals that have been bathed in the moonlight. If you can't access rainwater, use bottled spring water instead.

Goddess self-blessing

Anoint yourself with the water, and speak these phrases as a commitment to Self:

- ❖ I anoint my eyes, that they may see the beauty in the world.

- ❖ I anoint my mouth, that I may speak my truth with kindness.

- ❖ I anoint my ears, that they may hear and recognize love when it's spoken.

- ❖ I anoint my feet, that they may walk lightly on the Earth in reverence for all that is sacred.

Commit to honoring your body as a temple

You will need a pen and paper for this.

First, close your eyes and attune to your body with gratitude for all the things it does for you, 24/7. Then write a commitment of loving intent to honor your body as a temple. Here's an example:

'I hereby promise to speak only nice things to and about my body. I will prioritize my physical needs by noticing how certain foods make me feel, and ensure I eat and drink what leaves me feeling good. I will attend to my natural functions without delay, and only share my body with those who honor it with loving reverence.'

Divine embodiment

When you return home, go through your wardrobe and select any clothes that leave you feeling less than divine – such as 'desperation underpants'; items made from fabrics that don't allow your skin to breathe; garments that are ill-fitting or don't flatter your unique curves, or those that you associate with a difficult chapter in your life, imprinting a negative association. Put these in a bag and donate them to charity.

Then ask the universal light and love of the Goddess to send you some clothes that are more appropriate for your divine temple. Notice any inspired ideas or urges you have to take action, such as posting on social media your intent to manifest a Goddess wardrobe, visiting thrift shops, bartering with a seamstress friend, or holding a clothes swap to open channels for this intention to manifest.

SUMMARY

* A Goddess is a depiction or embodiment of the feminine as sacred in her own right, rather than a superhuman ideal of feminine perfection.

* Sacred feminine teachings and traditions are re-emerging after thousands of years of patriarchal conditioning that undermined the spiritual equality of the feminine.

* The feminine approach to time is through an understanding of the natural cycles and their influence, such as the cultural shifts created through the astrological ages.

* The dawning of the Age of Aquarius has seen women rise up to recover equal civil rights. It has now become a spiritual movement to reclaim sacred feminine traditions.

* Both men and women can be a force for global positive change when they honor their feminine traits and make self-honoring choices accordingly.

Yin reflection time

What images, thoughts, or ideas come to mind when you think of feminists? Are these stereotypes you've been fed by the media? What was life like for the women who spoke out and questioned the social roles afforded to them before the Women's Liberation Movement?

What personal experiences might have inspired them to make a difference? You may wish to take a moment to send your gratitude to those women who paved the way for the freedoms many of us now take for granted.

Chapter 2

Herstory: ancient Goddess cultures

Archaeological studies reveal that women enjoyed high status in early nomadic and agricultural societies, which recognized their feminine wisdom and power to create. Women were afforded respect as spiritual leaders in their communities, presiding over rituals of birth and death, and the observance of Mother Nature's cycles – information that was essential to the survival and wellbeing of all.[1]

Throughout the ancient world, the Mother Goddess was celebrated as the creator being,[2] and in Old Europe women were valued for providing 70 per cent of the food supply.[3] The collective sharing culture of the Goddess-worshipping communities who honored Mother Nature as the supreme provider disappeared with the advent of patriarchal societies, in which wealth was hoarded by the ruling class.

The evidence for Goddess cultures

During the patriarchal era, the concept of Goddess-worshipping communities was a hotly contested topic among archaeologists and anthropologists. Today, however, more and more evidence is coming to light to prove they existed. The Goddess is literally being unearthed.

As I write this chapter, another discovery has been made, at Poggio Colla in Tuscany, Italy: a stone tablet bearing 120 letters, including the name of Uni, an ancient fertility Goddess.[4] This will be used to reference a ceramic figurine found earlier at this archaeological site, which was once occupied by the Etruscans, the most powerful people in pre-Roman Italy. It depicts a woman in a squatting position, giving birth, and is one of 25,000 artifacts found there that reveal Goddess spirituality was central to Etruscan daily life.

It was once thought that ancient societies were primitive: their people godless heathens who behaved more like animals than civilized human beings. However, in the 1960s and 70s, this arrogant assumption was challenged by academics who re-introduced the concept of feminine spirituality. They used archaeological evidence[5] to demonstrate the existence of highly developed pre-patriarchal Goddess societies in which spiritual values governed the daily routines and laws adhered to by their citizens.[6]

Religion and creation myths

The ancient peoples of Sumer and Babylon (in Mesopotamia), Egypt, Africa, Australia, and China all had myths featuring a female deity as the creator of the world.[7] In fact, the sacred teachings and practices of the Goddess flourished for thousands of years in the Near and Middle East, long before the advent of the three main patriarchal religions – Judaism, Christianity, and Islam – which developed in the same area.

The biblical creation myth of Adam and Eve claims man was made in God's image and Eve was made for man. This established a core patriarchal belief that women exist for men, rather than as beings in their own right who are equally divine reflections.

While the Goddess has long been associated with the qualities of the Moon – such as reflection, intuition, and emotional maturity – some prehistoric cultures worshipped her as a Sun deity and had Moon gods who were considered of lesser importance. As I explained earlier, Sun Goddesses appeared in the mythologies of many cultures.

Those idol-worshipping pagans!

Most people are aware that the patriarchal religions forbade their followers to worship pagan idols. However, it isn't widely known that most pagan idols had breasts. With this understanding, it becomes clear that what was actually forbidden was the worship of the Goddess.[8]

Women's power and status

In ancient Greece, people worshipped Sophia as the Goddess of Wisdom. This is where we get the word 'philosophy': *philo*, meaning 'love of,' and *sophy*, meaning 'wisdom.' And Sophia's daughter, Athena, was invoked whenever a decision couldn't be reached in a court of law. Records have also been unearthed containing accounts of female magistrates and judges in northern Mesopotamia.

The pre-Christian Celts honored Cerridwen as the Goddess of Wise Counsel, while the Egyptians honored Maat as the Goddess of Divine Law and Order, and the Goddess Isis, who was said to have created those laws.[9] It was for this reason that, during the first 17 dynasties of ancient Egypt, queens were afforded more power than kings, and wives enjoyed higher social status and more freedom than their husbands.[10]

It was only in the 18th dynasty that the word 'pharaoh' was introduced, to describe the royal status of the male consort of the queen. This indicated the shift in power that resulted in the status of women being lowered.

Representations of the Goddess

Small, stylized statues of women that exaggerate the parts of the body associated with sexuality and fertility, such as the breasts and hips, have been found at numerous Paleolithic sites in western Europe – across Spain, France, Germany, Austria, and the Czech Republic – as well as Russia and India.[11] This indicates that the communities there revered women for their ability to gestate, birth, and nurture life. In Japan, 'Venus' pebbles carbon dated to 22,000BCE bear engravings of women.[12]

The sculptures of the Paleolithic and the later Neolithic periods were very similar in style, size, and materials, indicating a continuation of the sacred feminine spiritual worship and practices performed by nomadic hunting tribes right through to the civilizations that flourished after the advent of settled agriculture (see below).

As I mentioned earlier, archaeologists have traced Goddess worship back to 30,000BCE. However, American feminist historian Max Dashu has argued that female figurines found in Tan Tan, Morocco (dated 80,000–200,000BCE) and Berekhat Ram, Golan Heights (dated 230,000BCE) are even earlier depictions of the Goddess. They feature traces of red ochre, which suggests ritual use.[13]

At the Tell Arpachiyah site (in modern-day Iraq), female figures have been found featuring serpents, doves, and double axes – all symbols of the Goddess. Many of these were found in large circular rooms believed to be shrines. Some of the figures had vagina-shaped cowrie shells stained with red ochre, signifying people's reverence for the sacred life-giving blood that initiates women through their life transitions.

Perhaps the most spectacular Goddess-related prehistoric find to date was made in 1981 in northeastern Romania: a set of 13 Goddess figurines seated in circle around eight smaller figures. The larger Venus figurines are inscribed with symbols that archaeologist Marija Gimbutas documented in digs across Europe, including spirals, triangles, and chevrons – all of which are associated with ancient Goddess cultures.[14]

How Goddess cultures birthed civilization

According to the archaeological record, around 15,000 years ago*, in the hills where the Euphrates River flows into northern Syria, people discovered they could harvest the seeds of wild wheat.[15] So, instead of being constantly on the move, hunting and foraging, they could grow a staple food crop and store it for months, allowing them to settle in one area. The development of agriculture spread around the world over millennia, led by Goddess-worshipping people.

(*Recent evidence suggests agricultural activities may have been common in other parts of the world before 15,000 years ago. For example, it has been discovered that flour was milled from a native grass grain farmed by aboriginal Australians around 30,000BCE at Cuddie Springs, New South Wales. Early European explorers of the continent later documented that the flour produced the 'sweetest, lightest cakes they'd ever eaten.')[16]

Agriculture, and the vastly greater crop yields it produced, allowed people to live in permanent communities. As these thrived and expanded, an array of specialist arts and crafts developed, including pottery, basket weaving, leather craft, jewelry making, woodwork, stone carving, and painting. With survival no longer the immediate focus, creativity flourished.

This stable societal foundation enabled Goddess worship to evolve into an advanced religion, with symbols, mythologies, rituals, sacred lore, and practices. Ultimately, it also led to the emergence of the first great urban civilizations of the ancient world. The most advanced of these was Sumer, in Mesopotamia, but others existed during the Neolithic period in Crete, Cyprus, Anatolia, Palestine, and Jericho.

In Mesopotamia, the Goddess Ninlil was credited with having taught the people how to harness the natural cycles to create early agriculture. At Çatal Hüyük, an ancient Goddess settlement situated in what is now Turkey, archaeologists found gardening equipment such as hoes and sickles, in addition to storage jars for storing dry food and clay ovens.

The structure of Goddess societies

The Goddess-worshipping communities of prehistory were matrilineal, matriarchal, and matrifocal societies. To better understand these female-centered forms of social organization, let's briefly look at each in turn.

Matrilineal society

This is a system in which identity, property, and goods are passed through the maternal line, from mother to daughter. Matrilineal descent is referred to in Celtic mythology, suggesting the Celts themselves once traced lineage in this way.

Archaeologist Marija Gimbutas remarked on the gender equality evident in finds at Çatal Hüyük, one of the largest Goddess-worshipping sites ever discovered. These included over 40 separate altars to the three stages of womanhood. But she emphasized that the evidence suggested the society there was matrilineal.[17] Further evidence supporting the theory that early civilizations were matrilineal is provided by some of the surviving ancient tribes around the world today.

Anthropologists have suggested that early matrilineal cultures held a reverence for the feminine lineage because they did not comprehend the male role in conception. However, historian Tamara Griffiths disputes this assumption, saying:

'I personally don't believe early peoples didn't know the male role in conception. As hunters they needed to observe the breeding habits and cycles of animals. The argument that once people farmed animals the men knew how they were involved and patrilines took over, is spurious. I believe matrilines were used to identify lineages: there is physical evidence of motherhood, so interbreeding within a small population could be avoided.'

Women as providers

In 1946, British sociologist Viola Klein suggested that women held the balance of power in early societies because they generated the clan's source of wealth through the cultivation of crops and the provision of shelter through their matrilineal clan dwellings. Therefore, economically, men were dependent on women.

Matriarchal society

This is a form of social organization in which a woman is the head of a family, group, or state, and she, as the matriarch, is the recognized group leader who holds the governing power.[18] In a matriarchy, the choice to give a woman the mantle to rule is deliberate, rather than when a woman is offered rulership by default, such as in the absence of a male heir.

In Sumer, a civilization in Mesopotamia, the early kings (from 4500BCE) had to be willing to seek the counsel and blessing of the reigning high priestess, who was considered the representative of the Goddess on Earth. The king was regarded as the ruler of material matters and the priestess, the ruler of spiritual matters. That he ultimately deferred to her guidance signifies that the culture was matriarchal.

Ancient Sumerian fertility rites also demanded the sacrifice of the king if he was too old, frail, or impotent to fulfill his role in the annual fertility rites, or if he was too young and arrogant to defer to the counsel of the high priestess. No such limitations were imposed on the high priestess. Some claim kingly remains may have been used to fertilize crops.

The most celebrated king in ancient Mesopotamia was Sargon of Akkad,[19] whose mother was said to have been a high priestess and whose daughter became a priestess. He ruled for 40 years from 2334BCE and was a devotee of the Goddess Ishtar.

Warrior women

The Amazons are not figments of the imaginations of fantasy fiction writers. They were matriarchal tribeswomen of huntress warrior women living in Libya, Anatolia, Bulgaria, Greece, Armenia, and Russia.[20] In 49BCE, Diodorus of Sicily reported Amazon tribes in Libya who handed their children over to the men to be reared. In their culture, men were not permitted to hold public office and were relegated to domestic affairs – the way many women are in a patriarchal society.[21]

The latest forensic anthropology also reveals that a significant number of Viking warrior graves belonged to women known as 'shield maidens,' indicating they fought alongside their men. Welsh druidesses were also renowned for their battle strategies, and for their courage in defending their homes against Roman armies. Perhaps the most famous warrior woman of all was Boadicea, queen of the Iceni people of eastern England, who led a major uprising against occupying Roman forces.

....

Matrifocal society

This term is used for families and communities where one or more women do the majority of the child-rearing, with little or no input from the biological fathers. In many ancient cultures, women lived in multigenerational clans to share the task of child-rearing. The Neolithic period saw huge advances in social and material structures in which the offspring of a mother remained living in her house, thereby forming large 'clan families' that typically consisted of three or four generations living under the same roof.

From 5500BCE, these homes comprised numerous rooms situated around a central courtyard, indicating communal living. The courtyard was the area where the women performed their sacred ceremonies and baked bread, which was used in both their rituals and as a staple of their diet.[22]

Today, as the sacred feminine returns, we're seeing a rise in the matrifocal way of living in the form of single-parent households, predominantly headed by mothers. I predict that we'll eventually see government housing models emerge to support the growing number of sole parent families. These will feature multiple dwellings around a central multi-purpose building to promote shared child care, resources, and labor – the same model used in ancient matrifocal societies to provide support on all levels through the power of community.

The end of the Goddess era

By the third millennium BCE, the early Bronze Age, these advanced Goddess-centered civilizations had begun to fall. There were several factors that contributed to this. Around 2900BCE, warlike tribes living to the north of Old Europe started descending and conquering the region's peaceful, nature-worshipping communities.[23]

This shift was reflected in mythology: male heroes emerged who sought dominance over foreign lands and people. Rivalry for territory and power also made the early city-states in Asia and the Middle East increasingly militaristic, leading to the demise of Goddess-worshipping cultures there.

Another factor was the development of metallurgy. The manufacture of goods, including weapons, was transformed by the adoption of a strong new metal: bronze. This ushered in an era in which military force was used to amass greater authority and wealth. These influences led to the emergence of large empires whose rulers demanded allegiance to patriarchal ideologies and a state-endorsed religion that cast a male father God as the creator.

What next for matriarchy/patriarchy?

Just as some matriarchal societies viewed the male as the mere consort of the woman as Goddess, reducing his role to that of 'son/lover,' we have similarly seen patriarchal society view women as the subservient wife of the man who was made in God's image.

Having swung from matriarchy to patriarchy, the pendulum is now finding balance in each one of us as we learn to understand and value the role of both the feminine and masculine. This awareness is what will heal our unconscious need to diminish the other in order to assert our own importance and social status.

SUMMARY

❖ Archaeological evidence demonstrating the existence of ancient Goddess-worshipping civilizations continues to add weight to the prolific influence the Goddess wielded in the ancient world.

❖ There is evidence to show that some ancient Goddess cultures lasted for hundreds of years without war.

❖ Early Goddess communities were matriarchal, matrifocal and/or matrilineal. While many offered gender equality, others afforded women higher social status and freedoms than men.

❖ The development of agriculture enabled permanent settlements to form. This led to a flourishing of culture, and Goddess spiritual teachings and practices became an established and complex religious tradition.

❖ The demise of Goddess-worshipping cultures coincided with the development of metallurgy, which ushered in weapons that were used to amass status and power for the male rulers of empires.

Yin reflection time

Allow yourself to journey back in time and imagine how life must have been in those ancient Goddess communities: rearing children with the support of other women and living in an environment where women held positions of authority.

To do that, close your eyes and take your awareness into your blood – into the cells – and call upon your ancestors to reveal what life was like when the Goddess reigned. Take note of any images, sensations, or thoughts that surface.

Chapter 3
The Goddess tradition

When we gain access to the authentic wisdom and power of the sacred feminine teachings and practices that were once repressed, we often experience a feeling of homecoming. It's something we could always sense, but were not able to articulate. Given the lack of validation for the sacred feminine in our culture, this isn't surprising.

I've observed that once this veil is removed, many women experience a sense of personal empowerment. Gradually, they come to see how the distortion of the sacred feminine has impacted their development. I've also witnessed similar healing for men, whose development is stunted because their feminine expression is denied by patriarchal stereotypes.

Negative portrayals of the sacred feminine

Below is a list of the ways that the sacred feminine has been negatively portrayed, creating a distortion of the true feminine within our personal and collective psyche. This prejudice stunts the development of feminine traits within men and women, and our feminine identity and relationships as women.

1. Most of the faerytales that shape our psyche as young children portray elder women who practice magic as cold-hearted, evil, and manipulative witches and sorceresses.

2. Patriarchal religions offer us a dualistic reflection of womanhood, with icons of saintly, celibate mothers or lowly whores in need of redemption.

3. Most psychic phenomena on TV and in film is portrayed as terrifying and dark.

4. Intuitive insights are publicly dismissed in favor of rational proof.

5. The experiential wisdom of women is often ridiculed as 'old wives tales.'

6. Anyone who acknowledges the existence of other dimensional realities and beings, like faeries, is considered crazy.

7. In the past, practitioners of women-centered wisdom and spirituality were persecuted and killed: for example, during the witch hunts that took place in Europe between the 14th and 18th century.

Beyond the veil of illusion

The realization that it 'Ain't necessarily so' is like the moment in *The Wizard of Oz* when Dorothy catches a glimpse of the great wizard and discovers he's just a small man projecting an image that he's all powerful. Right then, she realizes she has given her personal power over to an illusion.

'The most powerful weapon in the hands of the oppressor is the mind of the oppressed.'
S<small>TEVE</small> B<small>IKO</small>

Awakening to the validity of the true feminine creates a shift within a woman's psyche that for many is profound and life changing. Clarity around this issue transforms and empowers a woman's perception of herself, which in turn instigates a healing of her internal shame and self-judgment, both conscious and unconscious.

Some women experience a temporary healing crisis as their established worldview breaks down, along with the persona they have carefully constructed. To assist the emergence of their authentic feminine expression, women need support to navigate the feelings of grief and anger that can surface when they realize how different their life could have been, had they received their birthright of women's wisdom to guide their choices.

How the Goddess tradition supports women

The teachings and practices of the sacred feminine offer us a supportive pathway to reconnect with our souls. They do this by weaving together the seemingly disparate aspects of our psyche, which include our shadow – our unseen and rejected side, which, if not positively integrated, can undermine our self-worth.

Women who have not been exposed to the parables and archetypes of the Goddess tradition often lack the insight and understanding of symbolism necessary to make sense of their experiences. This usually results in them trying to piece together a feminine sense of self by looking externally for cues. They observe what *others* value, and then construct a persona according to what they *think* will be pleasing to them. And in a patriarchal culture, that means disowning their feminine traits.

> *The Goddess tradition offers empowerment*
> *through self-awareness. This is summed up by*
> *the two words inscribed at the Goddess temple*
> *at Delphi in ancient Greece: 'Know thyself.'*

Mind versus heart

Those women who base their sense of self on an *external* reality will always feel disempowered, as they are dependent on constant reassurance and approval from others. Whereas those who are governed by their inner reality, feel an authentic sense of inner power and self-assurance based on their self-understanding and acceptance. These are the qualities that enhance our attractiveness to others.

Those who base their self-worth on the opinions of others are subjected to constant inner criticism and endless attempts to maintain their constructed persona. This is exhausting, and results in emotional mood swings and destructive behavior patterns such as yo-yo dieting, substance abuse, an obsession with celebrity gossip, compulsive spending, and cosmetic surgery – all of which keep women operating in a mindset of comparison and competition. This undermines our health and wellbeing on all levels, and impacts the quality of all our intimate and social relationships.

However, those women who have learned to attune to the *internal* guidance of their heart enjoy a sense of integrated wholeness and acceptance – toward themselves and others. This engenders patience and compassion, and reduces anxiety, depression, conflict, and destructive behavior.

This inner shift enables a woman to relax and express all of herself spontaneously, rather than feeling crippled by self-doubt due to the belief that she's imperfect and therefore unacceptable or unlovable.

Women whose feminine sense of self is wounded or disowned:

❖ Function predominantly from their rational mind.

❖ Try to be perfect in the roles they play, such as daughter, mother, employee, or lover.

❖ Feel pressure to live up to a conventional standard of beauty.

❖ May abandon their femininity to compete with men.

❖ May use their sexuality to gain love and acceptance.

❖ May use their appearance to exert power over men, and have their needs met.

❖ Lack the support to acknowledge their perceived imperfections; so they comfort themselves with food or substances.

✦ Compete with other women due to low self-worth and lack of authentic sisterhood.

Women whose feminine sense of self is empowered and embraced:

✦ Function predominantly from their heart.

✦ Understand that their intrinsic value has nothing to do with the roles they play.

✦ Appreciate their unique beauty and honor their body as a temple.

✦ Pursue their passion, ensuring they honor their needs in alignment with the natural cycles.

✦ Fill their cup with self-love and chose intimate partners with discernment.

✦ Identify and assert their needs directly, such as asking others in their community for assistance.

✦ Surround themselves with women who encourage them to accept and embrace their imperfections, thus reducing addictive behavior.

✦ Enjoy monthly sisterhood gatherings that strengthen their self-worth.

Exercise: Healing the inner critic

Think of a situation in your life where you're putting an expectation on yourself to be perfect – such as having the perfect body or pleasing others by being the perfect wife, mother, daughter, student, employee, boss, or role model. Alternatively, consider whether you place perfectionistic expectations on how well you perform a certain activity, such as your work tasks or your favorite hobby.

❖ Now take your awareness inside by closing your eyes. Ask yourself: 'What do I think I'll get in exchange for being perfect?' Open your eyes, and make a list of those pay-offs. Then ask yourself: 'Is this true?'

❖ Next, review your list of pay-offs and write down all the ways you can give yourself what you were hoping to get from *others* by being perfect. For example, if you were seeking love, make a list of self-loving actions you can take each week.

When we address our authentic core needs, we alleviate the pressure to be perfect.

Serving the sacred feminine

Below, I've documented the valuable roles that were once assigned to women who committed to serve the sacred feminine in society. Instead of being feared for using their natural gifts as women, they were respected. The omission of the sacred feminine from our society today has created an imbalance that now threatens all life on Earth. The good news is that we can all help to restore the sacred balance by re-introducing ancient feminine practices.

Wisdom keepers and teachers

Women's intuitive wisdom was once highly regarded. As stated earlier, in the advanced ancient cultures of Mesopotamia, kings sought counsel from the reigning high priestess. At the Oracle at Delphi in ancient Greece, pilgrims and nobles alike would seek guidance channeled by priestesses trained in divination.

Even after the patriarchy reassigned the temple to the God Apollo, political leaders in the ancient world – including Agamemnon, the king of Mycenae, Oedipus, the mythical king of Thebes, and Alexander the Great – sought the intuitive wisdom of the sacred feminine priestesses before committing troops to war campaigns.

In the modern world, we've lost the collaboration of masculine earthly power with feminine spiritual power. It was a partnership that ensured wise governance. The lack of feminine gnosis (inner knowing) in our halls of power has resulted in arrogant policies that place money above social and environmental sustainability.

Healers, herbalists, and midwives

Women were also once recognized for their healing abilities, but with the rise of the patriarchy, medicine became an elite science only taught to men of noble birth. The wise women who had administered to the health needs of the peasant classes were then considered such a threat to the growing medical establishment, that a genocide was committed between 1300 and 1600 CE.[2]

Women who had served their communities as healers and midwives were burned at the stake or drowned as witches. This directive served the political purposes of both the Church and the medical fraternity.

The handbook used to persecute women throughout Europe in the Middle Ages was the *Malleus Maleficarum* (translated as 'Hammer of the Witches'), authorized by Pope Innocent VIII in 1484. It outlined the Church's definition of what a witch did, and how she should be punished.[3]

In Salem, Massachusetts, USA in 1692–93, witch trials accused 150 people of witchcraft and executed 14 women. Led by Puritans, a religious movement that arose within the Church of England, they sought to 'cleanse' the wickedness inherent in women who had knowledge of the supernatural. This was based on the belief set out by the scriptures: Exodus 22:18 'Thou shalt not suffer a witch to live.'

There were exceptions, such as the Swiss physician and alchemist Paracelsus (1493–1541), who was one of the most influential scientists in early modern Europe. He claimed to have learned all he knew from the 'sorceresses,' and burned his pharmacopeia in protest at the persecution of herbalist women.[4]

Fortunately, as the sacred feminine returns, we are seeing the return of many ancient healing arts. But in response to this, a more covert witch hunt has been mounted by the medical establishment, in conjunction with pharmaceutical companies, who are attempting to suppress the prevalence of holistic therapies and complementary remedies, using fear campaigns and legislation to curtail their growing popularity.[5]

Sacred love arts and male initiation rites

In the Mesopotamian Epic of Gilgamesh, recognized as the oldest surviving great work of literature, the wild man Enkidu is civilized by a temple priestess trained in the love arts. She does this by initiating him into the teachings of the sacred feminine. The function of these dedicated temple priestesses was to initiate men through sacred sexual intercourse to awaken their kundalini (the life force essence that accelerates our consciousness).

When men returned from battle, these sacred women 'took the war out of them' by restoring their souls through acts of kindness and beauty. This ensured they were safe to return home to their families. Since all women in ancient Mesopotamia were required to perform at least one act of sacred sexual service as an act of devotion to the Goddess, there was no stigma around sex that meant it was anything less than sacred.

By contrast, in our modern world, where there's little reverence for the sacred power of sex, violence against women is at an all-time high, and the majority of men use pornography, which portrays acts of violence against women, to elicit sexual excitement.

Keepers of culture

Viewed as prostitutes by patriarchal historians, priestess women in the Goddess tradition were afforded high social status as the keepers of culture. Women of noble birth were selected for this honor and tutored in the sacred arts of poetry, dance, and music. Art and culture were prized as the mark of a truly great civilization, so kings sought to marry noblewomen who had cultivated an understanding and appreciation of great art.

In direct contrast, in a patriarchal society, academia and sport are afforded more value than art and culture. Consequently, in both the private and public sector, more funding is awarded to these pursuits than to the arts.

SUMMARY

❖ The sacred feminine has been negatively portrayed in popular culture and elsewhere, resulting in a wounded perception of and relationship with the feminine.

❖ When women gain access to authentic feminine wisdom, they start to heal the inner conflict caused by the rejection of the feminine.

❖ Women who *suppress* their feminine expression lead with their rational mind. This creates unrealistic expectations and self-criticism.

❖ Women who *empower* their feminine expression lead with their heart, which creates self-acceptance.

Yin reflection time

Take a moment before turning the page to consider how the portrayal of witches, step-mothers, and sorceresses has colored your perception of sacred feminine traditions. Imagine you were born in an alternate Universe in which you were exposed only to positive images of older women skilled in healing, wisdom, and energy work. If you had grown up in such a culture, how might you look and behave?

Part II

TEACHINGS AND PRACTICES

Chapter 4

Core beliefs and the three pathways of initiation

I'm going to play the role of your faery godmother for a moment...

Imagine I could wave my magic wand and grant you more energy. That would give you more patience with everyone around you, including yourself.

AND I could grant you the ability to know, ahead of time, the best windows to schedule everything from meetings to kids' parties, and from business launches to date nights – ensuring every social function and human interaction you have is a sparkling success!

AND I could tell you a secret that would enable your day-to-day life to feel more supported – and less of a constant struggle.

The secret is this: when we understand the ebb and flow of the natural cycles that govern us, we can plan our routines and activities accordingly. So, instead of pushing against the energetic tides and rhythms of life and wearing ourselves out, we go with the natural flow. Read on to discover how attuning to the natural cycles underpinned all the customs in the Goddess tradition.

Key customs in the Goddess tradition

Ultimately, what was honored most in the Goddess tradition was the cyclic wheel of life and death. This is reflected in every aspect of the ancient Goddess communities whose ruins have now been discovered. For example, to ensure sustainability and fertility, initiates were taught how to observe and understand the importance of each phase of the life cycle. This included honoring:

❖ The lunar, solar, and seasonal cycles as forces in the getting of wisdom.

❖ The sacred blood rites that initiate us, as women, into our life stages.

❖ Soul reincarnation; along with our ability to access past-life gifts and heal past-life karma in our current incarnation.

❖ Death and birth as the same sacred crossroads, each deserving equal reverence and support.

These core beliefs were reflected in sacred feminine practices, which harnessed:

❖ The power of ritual for setting intent and processing change.

❖ The power of community to create and sustain life.

- ❖ The power of art and trance states to bridge the inner and outer reality.

- ❖ The power of myths and archetypes to identify and integrate life lessons.

- ❖ The power of raising kundalini (life force) to expand consciousness and intuition.

We'll explore some of these practices in more detail later in the book. For now, let's take a look at a few other concepts that are recurring themes in the Goddess tradition.

The dying God and the birthing mother

Long before memorial days for fallen soldiers, or Mother's day, the ancients celebrated the heroic sacrifice of the dying God *and* the birthing mother. Yes – there were holy days to honor the contribution of both the sacred masculine and the sacred feminine, as these societies acknowledged that the cycle of life needed *both* aspects.

Women were honored for their sacrifices to serve the greater good, such as:

- ❖ Carrying and birthing new life.

- ❖ Nurturing and raising children.

- ❖ Growing food and ensuring spiritual growth for the wider community.

Men were honored for their sacrifices to serve the greater good. Such as:

- ❖ Losing their seed and life force in the act of procreation.

- ❖ Sacrificing their ego by being willing to submit to the annual soul descent journey.

- ❖ Risking their lives to hunt and protect on behalf of the tribe.

This ideology was based on the understanding that the balance of life is fragile, and that humans are dependent on the fertility created through the harmony of opposites – represented by Mother Earth and Father Sky working together in cyclic balance.

Honoring the creator/destroyer

Just as birth and death (creator/destroyer) are honored as equally sacred in the Goddess tradition, so too are the light and the dark. It's understood that each contains the other, like the Chinese yin/yang symbol. When we acknowledge both aspects within us, we can take responsibility for them and develop ways to balance our polarities.

For example, when we understand that the Full Moon always occurs in the opposite zodiac sign to the sign the Sun is in, we can identify the exact traits we need to balance within ourselves to minimize tension and conflict. Conflict is created through polarization, whereas harmony is created through balance.

The many faces of the God and Goddess

Just as there are a variety of life forms in nature, the Goddess path seeks to honor the divine in every facet of existence, including us. This is why it's considered a polytheistic religion (having many deities): it recognizes the many aspects of the God and Goddess that comprise the whole.

When we understand that Goddess myths are parables that portray universal human dramas, and that the Gods and Goddesses who feature in them are aspects of our own psyche, it becomes apparent that they serve as a map for self-understanding. The various deities represent all of our seemingly disparate parts. Through their stories we learn how to integrate the full scope of human expression. They are not simply an array of separate entities who are externally worshipped.

A Goddess by any other name

All over the world, people celebrated the many faces of the God and the Goddess. Despite variations in geographical location and names, the deities shared similar myths and archetypal qualities. Why? These aspects are within our collective consciousness, which explains why the same symbolic images are used to depict the God and Goddess archetypes, regardless of cultural variation.

Reflection and embodiment of the divine

The Goddess tradition sees everything as inherently divine. This viewpoint encourages us to identify the blessing and lesson in every situation. The focus is on attaining personal mastery through self-awareness, so rather than seeking to please an external deity, we fulfill our divine potential through self-enquiry and observation.

This is why divination tools such as oracles are employed to help discern and identify one's personal lesson in a given situation. This is the path of the mystic: one who seeks union with the divine through direct experience, rather than through an intermediary, such as a vicar or a rabbi. This affirms our intrinsic connection with existence.

Sexuality: a path to union with the divine

The Goddess tradition doesn't view sexuality as profane or dirty. It perceives our sexual energy as our life force. When awakened and directed with conscious intent, it offers us a pathway to expand our consciousness and bridge our spiritual and physical nature.

This is why there are yogic practices in the Goddess tradition to 'awaken the serpent of light': the Goddess essence that resides in the central nervous system contained within our spinal cord. This reverence for the power of human sexuality is why some initiates chose to devote themselves to awakening kundalini through acts of sacred union, such as yoga and Tantra (we'll look at these practices later in the book).

The power of three and the triple Goddess

The number three and multiples of three are considered a potent combination in the Goddess tradition, as they represent the divine trinity of:

❖ Maiden, Mother, Crone (the three stages of womanhood)

❖ Knight, King, Sage (the three stages of manhood)

❖ Past, present, future

❖ Mother, father, child

The archetypal wise woman Goddess, the Crone, is often shown with three faces, just as her domain, the Underworld, was guarded by Cerberus, a three-headed dog. This feature denotes one who has knowledge of all three aspects of life, which grants them deep sacred knowledge.

The three worlds

The Goddess tradition acknowledges that life is multidimensional – existing simultaneously on numerous planes. For example, the Norse people, who worshipped both the sacred feminine and masculine, believed that three worlds existed within Yggdrasil, the World Tree (see below). This consisted of an upper world, an everyday world, and the Underworld. Rather than physical destinations, these are states one traverses within the inner planes of existence.

The Tree of Life

The 'Tree of Life' was a widespread sacred concept in Goddess-worshipping societies. A metaphysical tree, it represented an inner path of ascension that an aspirant could traverse through dedicated intent and disciplined spiritual practices.

For instance, if someone engaged in ecstatic yogic or ritual practices, they would climb the tree within and transcend the everyday world, experiencing the upper world with the expanded presence of a deity.

This was how ancient Tantrikas (priestesses of the Goddess) in the Indus civilization, the earliest known urban culture in India, were able to channel the sacred teachings and practices to help others embody their true divine nature.

The everyday world represented the present, in which we encounter the karmic repercussions of our actions. The Underworld was the void within, revered as the womb of rebirth in the Goddess tradition.

Supernatural phenomena

The Goddess tradition doesn't dismiss the spirits who dwell in the other kingdoms as mere make-believe. Instead, it encourages us to perceive other dimensional beings by refining our energy field, and attuning to them through our subtle senses.

This is why ancient legends depicted heroes who respected or even feared the elemental beings. These are the Mythic creatures that exist within our inner landscape, such as elves, gnomes, sprites, brownies, dryads, fauns, and unicorns.

In the myths in which a mortal man married a Goddess, he would lose her if he didn't respect her need to periodically return to the Underworld to restore her magical essence. So too, women who become disconnected from the mystic realm often struggle with the mundane demands of marriage and motherhood, and enter depression if their soul self isn't nourished.

Magical menstruation

The patriarchal culture views women's menses as toxic waste, unlike the Goddess tradition, which considers it holy: it is seen as the life-filled substance from the womb of the Goddess, with the power to restore life. In addition to its physical potency, menstruation was revered for its energetic power: menstrual blood was used in ceremonies and to consecrate fertility amulets and burial mounds.[1]

We're now starting to reverse the association of menstrual blood with death, instead of life. Scientists are using menstrual-derived stem cells to treat disease,[2] and more mothers ensure their daughters receive an initiation into the ancient tradition of the Moon Lodge: a sacred space in which women gather at New Moon to honor their potential for rebirth during their menstruation.

Doing what comes naturally

Those on the Goddess path seek to live as close to nature as possible. This stems from the understanding that nature evokes our soul, unlike urban environments, which can breed egoic arrogance as we compare and compete with others.

Living in nature creates a sense of relaxed acceptance of one's nakedness and bodily functions. Nature also encourages us to honor both the Earth Mother and our bodies with healthy choices, such as whole foods and organic remedies and skin care.

Live like a Goddess by creating a divine life

In order to have a divine life, one must strive to align with the divine design of nature – the spiral. You may know this as the Fibonacci sequence: the elegant mathematical equation in which each number equals the sum of the preceding two numbers, creating a spiral. It can also be understood as 'what was' plus 'what is' creates 'what will be' – the Universal Law of Reciprocity known colloquially as 'cause and effect.'

The spiral occurs repeatedly in nature: it can be seen in the matrix of pinecones, sunflowers, fern fronds, and nautilus shells. Everything in nature is cyclic, from our spiraling DNA to the seasons and the life cycle of every living being. So when we structure our lives in accordance with the ebb and flow of the cycles of nature, our life becomes more sustainable on all levels.

And when we understand the effect natural cycles have on our moods, energy levels, creativity, and libido, we can maximize that in our favor, by scheduling our routines so we're 'in sync' with nature (in Chapter 7 I offer practical tips on how to do that). Linear time induces stress and an unhealthy expectation that we must always be 'on.' We expect ourselves to behave as digital machines, rather than organic beings.

The sacred spiral of life

The Goddess tradition teaches us how to honor the natural cycles as pathways to maturity and wisdom (I describe these below in the 'three pathways of initiation'). It also instructs us in how to consciously direct energy for a specific purpose and intent by gathering 'in circle' and generating a vortex of power during significant celestial alignments.

We've been taught to fear magic through cultural superstitions that insist we can't be trusted with our own power. In the Goddess tradition we are taught to respect the power of magic, which is simply the conscious use of our energy. This is one of the ways that the Goddess path encourages us to be responsible and aware of the effects of our actions.

Since cyclic energy moves in spirals, it can ascend or descend – as can we. If we make life-affirming choices, our life becomes an upward spiral of energy, promoting growth and enlightenment. And if we make self-negating choices, our life becomes a never-ending struggle – a downward spiral.

It's inevitable that we experience both upward and downward spirals because life initiates us with unexpected challenges. So the Goddess tradition teaches us how to navigate these vortices by consciously embracing and understanding each cycle. This awareness reduces the fight-or-flight response, helping us to stay centered and identify our lesson, moment-to-moment, by attuning to our intuition. This promotes self-reliance and governance.

Understandably, a downward spiral can be terrifying if we don't understand the terrain. It's normal to fear the unknown, so we're more likely to panic and feel overwhelmed if we don't understand the 'descent journey.'

Common causes of a downward spiral

The following are life experiences that can initiate a downward spiral:

1. Grief when a relationship ends.

2. The seasons of autumn/winter, when there's less solar light, resulting in less energy.

3. Illness/injury.

4. Menstruation.

5. Transitions such as puberty, pregnancy, parenthood, mid-life, menopause, empty nest syndrome, or moving into an aged care facility.

Dealing with a downward spiral

The following practices can help us navigate a downward spiral:

1. Creative self-expression, such as poetry, painting, and composing music, helps us transmute negative experiences into works of beauty and wisdom through accessing the language of our soul. Art helps us heal and integrate trauma by recording our inner landscape; this helps us make sense of the dark and return to the light.

2. Parables and myths help us identify our archetypal lessons and provide a map to integrate disassociated aspects of our psyche (these are coming up in Chapter 8).

3. Simple self-created rituals help us to set clear intent, anchor changes, and surrender to a higher power – by invoking insight and guidance (we will explore some rituals in Chapter 9).

4. Dream analysis and oracles help us consciously understand the messages from our subconscious, and act as keys to new ways of seeing (more on this in Chapter 11).

5. Sacred bathing (explained in Chapter 9) and guided meditations help us enter the stillness, so we're receptive to intuitive insights.

Exercise: Enter the spiral to reclaim your power

To reframe the spiral journey of descent in your life into a powerful
initiation, try the following process. You'll need a pen and a blank sheet
of paper.

❖ Begin by drawing a large spiral on the paper. Now recall the most
   challenging experience you've ever had. Don't edit yourself: go with
   the first one you think of, as that's the one being offered by your
   intuition.

❖ Now, start at the outside of your spiral, and write along the curved
   line, detailing the sequence of events and the feelings that took you
   on your journey of descent via destruction and chaos.

❖ Once you arrive in the middle of your spiral, take a moment to sit
   with your eyes closed. Consider what lessons you learned from that
   experience.

❖ Now start to write those lessons along the inside of the curved line,
   as you retrace your way out of the spiral.

Analysis time!

You can use this process to find the hidden gems in any challenging
situation you encounter. It illustrates how, periodically, life initiates us
into the unknown, and how the key to becoming wise is to stop and
reflect on the inherent gifts and blessings we gain from each descent
journey. The more we consciously embrace each descent, the less
we fear the unknown and develop a trust in our own intuition and the
process of life.

The three pathways of initiation

The Goddess tradition offered three distinct spiral pathways of initiation to help people live in harmony with the three main energy cycles that impact the human psyche and relationships – the lunar, solar, and seasonal cycles.

All three pathways involve a spiral 'journey of descent,' for it's by descending to our depths and facing our fear of the unknown that we retrieve the lost fragments of our psyche. We then spiral back up to experience a rebirth.

The solar, lunar, and seasonal descents

In the ancient world, initiates undertook the three pathways – the solar, lunar, and seasonal descents – to become wise, whole, and healed, so they could return to serve the greater good as clear vessels for divine will. This is what it means to walk the path of the Goddess: undertaking a commitment to restore all the disparate aspects of our soul.

Initiates who consciously undertook descent journeys within the Goddess temples were revered for their willingness to embody the aspect of the 'dying God.' This involved submitting to a process called an 'ego death' – a personal crisis encountered when the stakes are high and our life doesn't match our desires. It is then that we must learn to surrender to a higher power. This instigates a shift in which we are directed by the soul, rather than the rational mind.

Those who returned from this perilous descent journey as a resurrected Goddess or God were greeted with great fanfare. They were celebrated as a true heroine/hero who had risked all to return with fresh insights though their meeting with the Goddess within.

We'll be exploring descent journeys in more depth in the following chapters, but here's a brief overview of them.

1. The solar descent
Unveiling the seven faces, or aspects, of the God/Goddess

This pathway of initiation, which is also known as the solar descent journey of the Maiden, is undertaken through autumn and winter, when the solar light wanes. This instigates a meeting with our shadow: our inner aspects that are not acknowledged, understood, or integrated.

It's an inner journey in which the initiate confronts everything they have rejected or disowned about themselves. It involves a guided descent to meet each of the seven universal feminine aspects that govern the seven chakras and together comprise our feminine psyche (we'll explore this in Chapter 5, Shakti power).

Through meeting each of the Goddess aspects who govern the chakras, we unveil our illusory beliefs and learn to discern our deepest truth, and know, accept, and love our true self. The solar descent journey enables a woman to transition from princess to queen. Alumni would then return to unveil their masculine aspects, to become whole. Men also did this descent, unveiling their masculine, then their feminine aspects – a process which helped them mature and embody the archetypal King.

Unveiling the bride

Have you ever wondered where this wedding custom comes from? Its origins lie in the solar descent journey of the Maiden. It was a practice undertaken by noblewomen in preparation for marriage. Unless a bride-to-be had unveiled all the aspects of her soul at each of the seven chakras (you'll learn about this in the next chapter), she wasn't able to unveil her true self for her beloved.

The descent of Ishtar

This solar descent journey of the Maiden is detailed in the ancient Babylonian myth of Ishtar (known as Inanna in Sumer, Mesopotamia). Ishtar is the queen of Heaven who descends to the Underworld to help her sister, Ereshkigal, give birth. Like anyone entering the Great Below, Ishtar is stripped bare of her previous identity and confronted with her greatest fears. In her vulnerability she invokes help from above.

This act of conscious surrender catalyzes Ishtar's return as the resurrected Goddess. On arriving home, she discovers that her immature partner has been smoking a reed pipe in her absence. So she initiates him into maturity by sending him to the Underworld – this is why Ishtar was said to be 'the maker of kings.'

The ancient Greek tale of Psyche, who descends to the Underworld in search of true love, is another example of the solar descent journey of the Maiden. In ancient Greece, seven maidens and seven youths were 'sacrificed' in the annual labyrinth journey. This referred to those who descended through the chakras to meet their ego and overcome it.

2. The seasonal descent

Relationship descent and resurrection

This path of initiation is undertaken by the initiate priest-king or priestess-queen, one who has completed the solar descent. It involves observing the life lessons evoked by the turning of the seasonal wheel, known as the Wheel of Eight: you'll learn about this in Chapter 6.

This is the practice of sacred relationship: a shared path of descent undertaken by the Holy Couple – graduates of the solar descent who had entered into partnership or parenthood. Through completing the lessons of each gateway on the Wheel of Eight, initiates would learn to grow together gracefully by honoring every phase in the circle of life.

This descent completes the full circle of yin and yang, as initiates explore the inward phase of separation from their lover by embracing intimacy with their inner self during the autumn/winter, followed by the outward phase of union and shared intimacy during the spring/summer. This practice of conscious relating develops and supports sustainable and interdependent relationships, families, and communities.

The star of Ishtar

The eight-pointed star known as the 'star of Ishtar' symbolized this cyclic journey of the lovers. It was valued by the ancients, who revered the sacred journey above and below as a means of creating true power and abundance. The star of Ishtar symbol was featured on Greek coins and on stone and clay reliefs created by the Sumerians, the Assyrians, the Babylonians, and the Hittites in Mesopotamia.

The ancient Aztec calendar also featured a Sun with eight rays, and the Crescent Moon and eight-pointed star later became the symbol of Islam. However, the star of Ishtar was originally a symbol that honored the seasonal descent journey of the God and Goddess. It was said that completion of this rite established a person as a noble who could wear the symbol of the Crescent Moon under the eight-pointed star to signify their social status as a priest-king or priestess-queen.

3. The lunar descent

The journey of the 13 Moons

This descent journey was undertaken in the womb sanctuary of the Red Tent/Moon Lodge – the place where women gathered during New Moon. It was considered a preparation for one's elder phase, and involved consciously journeying with the lunar cycle. Over 13 consecutive lunar months, initiates sought to embrace their shadow traits and observe the lesson of each zodiac sign during the darkest phase of the Moon: the time when our unhealed aspects surface.

This path was considered a shamanic journey to activate one's full feminine power and wisdom. Often, those called to this path went on to train as ceremonial priestesses, assisting women with their psychological deaths and rebirths at each of their life transitions. These rites of passage were also conducted within the Red Tent.

The 13 Clan Mothers

Indigenous peoples in North America once referred to their land as 'Turtle Island,' a name that stemmed from the belief that they were riding on the back of the Great Mother, who they called Mother Turtle. One legend told how Mother Turtle carried the 13 stories of the Moon on her back.

These teachings were said to have been gifted by the original grandmothers, the Clan Mothers of the original 13 tribes. These wise women were revered as luminescent star beings who had incarnated to teach women's medicine within the Moon Lodge.[3]

The 13 Moons lunar practice was also undertaken in the Hindu tradition, which honored the dark Goddess and the integration of one's shadow. People understood that when the New Moon was in each zodiac sign, it illuminated the lessons of each segment of the zodiac, which they referred to as a 'lunar mansion.' Through understanding and mastering the mythic story of each sign, one would accumulate personal medicine or healing power.

The mother as spiritual teacher

Ancient societies honored women's role as spiritual teachers. A role that was essential for each child's development if he or she was to become a contributing member of the tribe. The mother was acknowledged as a child's first spiritual teacher.

Why? For the first seven years of our life, our mother teaches us to follow the patterns of nature in order to grow our independence. For example, she advises us to keep warm in winter and drink enough water in summer. This life stage is when we're most dependent on our mother as our primary carer. It's when we're instilled with feminine values, such as sharing, inclusion, and honoring feelings.

From the age of seven our focus inevitably shifts from the feminine to the masculine, as we explore the outer world and start to develop our ego. So we seek feedback from authority figures like teachers, and emulate what we see in the media. In a patriarchal society we soon observe that feminine values aren't the way of the world, so we often abandon them in order to survive.

> 'Give me a child until he is seven, and I will show you the man.'
> ARISTOTLE, GREEK PHILOSOPHER

While it may be difficult for mothers to feel dismissed or disrespected by their children, we must remember that the foundations have been laid and we have great power as women to shape the future by teaching our children how to live in alignment with the natural world. The ancient agricultural communities who worshipped the natural cycles knew their lives depended on them.

Our current global ecological crisis is now reminding us that we must return to living symbiotically with nature. This awareness will restore a deeper respect for the wisdom of the feminine and the status of the mother as the soul's first spiritual teacher.

The seven-year cycles in our life journey

In order to grow and assist others to grow, it's helpful to understand the lessons we face as we experience the lesson of a different chakra every seven years (the chakras are explained in the next chapter). This teaching has survived from the Goddess-worshipping Vedic tradition, although mystic traditions like the Tarot also observe this cyclic series of lessons.

0–7 years: innocence

During the first seven years of our life, our mother is usually our primary influence as we learn to develop awareness and responsibility for our physical self-care; this is based on applying cyclic routines like washing and eating. It's at this age that we develop feminine qualities like sharing, creativity, and imagination.

7–14 years: exploration

At the age of seven we start to develop our persona, based on the social cues we receive and interpret from those around us. This is when we become more focused on attaining our father's attention and approval. So we develop more masculine qualities and seek to achieve results, hone specific skills, and assert our thoughts and opinions.

14–21 years: connection

In our teens, our peers become our primary focus as we seek greater connection with those outside our primary family of origin. This is when we start to ponder our potential and our ability to create and make a difference in the world.

21–28 years: individuation

This stage marks the end of our youth and our dependence on our parents as we pursue a path of our own making. This is a time of courage and self-belief that's often referred to as the 'bold confidence of youth.'

28–35 years: commitment

During these years we often put down roots by making a commitment to a career, a relationship, or a property. This is when we feel the urge to create something enduring, so we have something substantial to show for our efforts.

35–42 years: service

In this phase we're often caring for others or investing in a future legacy with the energy we've learned to generate, sustain, and conserve.

42–49 years: surrender

This mid-life period is often a time of personal re-evaluation and self-examination. We may experience a healing crisis, unexpected loss, or a life change that acts as a catalyst to shift our perceptions.

49–55 years: being

Our primary challenge in this phase is to accept 'what is' and find the blessing in the present moment, developing a sense of communion with all of existence.

Post-55 years: innocence

Our lesson is to complete the cycle by returning to a state of innocence and trust.

SUMMARY
. . . .

❖ To create more ease and less stress, we need to align with the ebb and flow of the natural cycles.

❖ In life, we can spiral up or down, depending on our choices and challenges. The Goddess tradition offers practical processes to help us return from the chaos of descent spirals with insight and a fresh perspective.

❖ The Goddess tradition acknowledges spirit in everything – including ourselves as multidimensional spiritual beings, having a human experience.

❖ The ancient Goddess-worshipping civilizations honored three pathways of initiation. These helped people mature in alignment with the solar, seasonal, and lunar cycles.

❖ A mother was once honored as the spiritual teacher who taught her children how to live symbiotically with nature. This awareness is returning as we acknowledge the cost of a culture that denies this nature-based wisdom.

Yin reflection time

Pause to reflect on your relationship with time. Do you feel constant pressure to fit as much as possible into every hour of every day, as if you're a machine? When was the last time you stopped to reflect on a sunset at the end of a day, or went for a moonlit walk at Full Moon?

Consider how you can do more to embrace the seasons in your life – by undertaking activities such as a detox cleanse or de-cluttering your home to move old energy during the changing seasons of spring and autumn.

Chapter 5
Shakti power

Within our bodies is a current of bioelectrical energy. It's our animating force, our sacred essence. The ancient Goddess-worshipping peoples of India called it 'Shakti.' It's also known as kundalini or 'serpent power' because it lies coiled around the base of our spine like a serpent – dormant until it's activated.

Shakti power is the Goddess essence we awaken within our nervous system when we unveil the seven Goddesses who govern our chakras in the solar descent journey. On hearing the truth of these sacred teachings, our sacred feminine energy meridian rises like a serpent being charmed by the sound of a wooden flute played with sacred intent...

Raising the serpent

The process described above is what's known as 'Shaktipat,' an energetic transmission that electrifies our codes of remembrance and jolts our soul into a state of awakened or expanded awareness. This soul awakening is often experienced as an ecstatic trance state in which we feel the bliss of unification with all of existence, and remember ourselves as eternal.

Ideally, we'll have this spiritual awakening in a place where we feel safe, held, and supported, as we would also hope for our initiation into menstruation or our sexual awakening – for example, at a retreat or on a course run by an experienced facilitator who is able to help us integrate the experience.

In order to safely raise our kundalini energy, it's imperative that we are clear and grounded physically. This creates a foundation for integrating the experience with conscious understanding and unifying practices. In this way, we can balance our human identity with our divine identity – which is the purpose of physical incarnation.

Exercise: Extracting Soma

Kundalini is our inner fire, so when we actively raise it, we need to balance the energy with deep states of relaxation. This soothes our nervous system so we don't become manic or quick to anger. This cooling energy is called Soma. It's the essence we extract from moments of pleasure and beauty.

To cultivate Soma, take yourself on a walking meditation in nature and imbibe the natural beauty you observe through your five earthly senses. For example, inhale the scent of blossom; attune to the sensation of the air on your skin or the grass or sand beneath your feet; see the colors of the changing leaves or the sky scape at dawn; listen to the sound of birdsong, and taste the rain on your tongue.

The seven chakras

To activate our Shakti power we need to embody within our psyche, one by one, the seven faces – or aspects – of the Goddess that govern the seven major 'chakras.' This allows us to gradually integrate the energetic shifts of awakening kundalini within our central nervous system, while consciously processing the expanded consciousness this generates.

The chakras are psychic-energy centers within our body – chakra is a Sanskrit word meaning 'wheel,' and the chakras are often called 'wheels of light.' In the ancient world, they were also known as the 'Seven Eyes of God' as they open our awareness of the seven states of consciousness.

There are seven major chakras: six located roughly along the spinal cord, and another one located just above the crown of the head. The diagram below shows the location of the seven chakras and the colors associated with them; each color reflects a type of vibration or frequency radiating through the chakra.

Here's a brief description of the function of each chakra:

Base (red): governs our physical body

Sacral (orange): governs our emotional body

Solar plexus (yellow): governs our lower mental body

Heart (green): governs our psyche (Soul)

Throat (blue): governs our etheric (energy) body

Third eye (indigo): governs our higher mental body

Crown (violet): governs our cosmic body

The chakras

The rainbow bridge

When a chakra is fully 'open' – spinning and functioning well – we enjoy health on all levels. A fully open chakra emanates one of the seven color rays (as seen on the diagram); when all seven are open, we radiate our full spectrum of light – like a rainbow bridge. This is why Ishtar, the queen of Heaven, and Lilith, the earthly serpentine Goddess of kundalini, who resided in the branches and roots of the mystical Tree of Life, were said to wear rainbow necklaces, indicating their activated rainbow bridge.

So too, when our inner Tree of Life is fully lit up, we become a conduit for the energy of the sacred feminine. This process awakens our serpent power (kundalini) from the base to the crown, which activates the self-aware and sovereign queen within who embodies all Goddess aspects.

The seven chakra Goddesses

Each of the seven chakras is governed by one of the seven aspects of the Goddess – the universal archetypes that provide a map of our feminine psyche. When we understand the strengths and lessons of each Goddess aspect, we can express them confidently in our life. When all seven aspects are empowered, we feel whole, and do not need to search for someone to 'complete' us.

The seven Goddess aspects act as 'keys' for opening the seven chakras. As we embody each of the Goddess aspects, we open a chakra, emitting a strong, vibrant color in our energy field. The process of empowering the seven chakra Goddesses is complex, so it's best done under the guidance of an experienced facilitator who can assist you to do this with adequate support in working through the shadow – the unseen and rejected side – of each aspect. (See Goddess archetypes in Resources section.)

However, below I've given a brief overview of the seven Goddess aspects. You'll probably recognize some more than others in yourself, depending on which ones were encouraged and mentored in your early life. If you observe the lessons outlined here, you'll be on your way to empowering your seven inner Goddesses!

Base chakra: Lilith, the wild woman

When our inner wild woman is empowered we feel comfortable with our natural selves, and with most base forms of expression such as lust and anger. We honor anger as a feeling that prompts us to take some kind of action, often because we feel unsafe. If we are uncomfortable with acknowledging our feelings of anger, we can be dominated by others, or instead, manipulate them with passive-aggressive behavior.

If we fail to speak up, for fear of rejection or generating conflict, we diminish our personal power and passion. Having an empowered wild woman means we're able to be authentic in any situation and be uninhibited in our erotic expression.

Sacral chakra: Aphrodite, the beautiful muse

Aphrodite is the Goddess of Love, so when she's operating positively in our psyche we generate self-love by making self-honoring choices. But if our self-love is lacking, shadow Aphrodite will surface. Examples of shadow Aphrodite behavior include using glamour to seduce others in a bid to convince ourselves we're beautiful and lovable; falling in love with emotionally unavailable people; and getting enmeshed in serial dramas.

When our inner Aphrodite is empowered, we're emotionally mature. So we're less likely to experience huge emotional swings or comfort eat as a way of soothing our sensitivity.

Solar plexus chakra: Athena, the golden heroine

This Goddess archetype is the most masculine because she governs our rational mind. She's the part of us that wants to prove our worth by achieving some measure of success. If we have low self-worth, no amount of success will be sufficient to compensate for our wound. This often leads women to operate out of shadow Athena, and become workaholics.

When our inner Athena is functioning well, we're assertive, organized, happy for others to succeed, and committed to taking calculated risks to achieve our goals. The key to strengthening this aspect lies in acknowledging consistent effort via a step-by-step plan, and having a life outside of work so our job doesn't define us. Those who are married to the job often incur illness as a wake-up call.

Heart chakra: Demeter, the Earth empress

Our archetypal mother governs our heart center. This is the part of us that ensures our needs are met. Without it, we're not centered enough to bring anything to fruition, or to sustain nurturing (of ourselves or others). The heart is the center of self-acceptance, so if this chakra isn't open, we judge ourselves, and others, harshly for not being perfect.

When this chakra is open, we allow and accept our imperfections, understanding that they're often our greatest teachers. When our inner Demeter is empowered, we create a welcoming home and enjoy spending time there to center and rejuvenate. One of our greatest Demeter lessons is to honor the fact that change is inevitable and that everything has its season – whether we're birthing a creative project or tending a garden. Once our creation is fully grown, we must honor its need for independence.

Throat chakra: Artemis, the medicine woman

This aspect is the lone wolf or Amazon who tends to prefer the company of her sisters while healing her past wounds. Since this chakra is the gateway to the upper energy centers, our challenge here is to see our wounding from a higher perspective. We can then appreciate our specific issues for the lesson they can teach us. When we heal, we avoid shutting down and armoring up in anticipation of further wounding.

When this aspect is empowered we realize that our ultimate healing comes through forgiveness. We also trust ourselves to set clear boundaries that honor our vulnerability. Expressing our inner self and reconnecting with our feelings helps us stay emotionally available – to ourselves and to others.

Third eye chakra: Hecate, the wise woman

Hecate is the archetypal wise woman who resides in us all, regardless of our age. She's the part of us that feels reclusive and enjoys meditation, esoteric study, and sacred ceremony. When she operates in the shadows, we suffer bouts of depression and have no access to a mystical perspective to make sense of our darker thoughts, feelings, and experiences. If the third eye chakra is shut down, we dismiss psychic phenomena out of fear or ignorance.

Our inner Hecate reclaims her power when we acknowledge the wisdom we've gained through all our 'down times.' When she's empowered we use our intuitive insights to help others make sense of their shadowlands journeys. When Hecate is disempowered, we fear aging and death.

When she's empowered, we let out our eccentricities – without fear of persecution by those who feel threatened by a different perspective.

Crown chakra: Ishtar, the high priestess

The aspect who governs our crown center is Ishtar, the Tantrika. Her lesson is to embody our divine essence in the world through sacred intent and practices. When this archetype is disempowered we don't 'walk our talk' when it comes to our spiritual values. If we disconnect from Ishtar we'll unconsciously prostitute our energy by doing jobs that drain us in exchange for money. We'll also choose partners for security, rather than because the connection is soul-fulfilling.

When our inner Ishtar is empowered, we're sovereign and self-fulfilling – a queen unto ourselves. We're discerning when choosing our partners, only considering those who are capable of acknowledging, and taking responsibility for, their strengths *and* weaknesses.

Challenging chakras

Without exception, those who have undertaken the process of activating the seven inner Goddesses with me at my Goddess retreats and via my online courses always find that the throat and third eye chakras are the most challenging. Why is this?

The throat chakra stirs up our core wounds, including betrayal of sisterhood and our deepest feelings of shame. The third eye is where we enter the void: the place of chaos where we must learn to surrender. It's only when we arrive at the crown chakra that everyone in the group feels the harmonic resolve that marks a time of great personal victory and celebration!

If you're interested in activating your seven chakra Goddesses you may wish to look into the online and live events I facilitate, or read my workbook *The Inner Goddess Makeover*. Details can be found at my website: www. themoonwoman.com

Ten reasons to activate your Goddess mojo

Here are the main benefits of opening our chakras by activating our inner Goddesses:

1. We unleash our creative energy.

2. We create a clear channel for intuitive insights.

3. We gain access to past-life memories.

4. We perceive things beyond the physical senses through our subtle senses.

5. We have more vitality, which magnetizes people to us.

6. We experience greater longevity, and appear youthful.

7. Our libido and sexual magnetism is increased.

8. We can access altered states without the aid of substances.

9. We can connect to our authentic voice of truth in all situations.

10. We feel connected to existence, and as a result, have no fear of change or death.

The path to queendom

While this process of empowering the seven feminine archetypes marks the solar descent of the Maiden aspect within us, it's never too late to take the journey. It provides the getting of wisdom needed to build a solid foundation for relationships, since all our interactions are a reflection of our relationship with ourselves.

Time and time again while initiating people through the solar descent, I'd witness women of all ages arrive at the initial sessions wearing tailored, masculine clothes and lots of make-up. Then, as they discovered the full spectrum of feminine expression, they would soften, start growing their hair out and wearing flowing, feminine clothes. This indicated their acceptance and appreciation of their feminine sense of self.

In the ancient world, those who awakened their 'serpent power' from the base to the crown were honored as spiritual leaders; this is illustrated in the cobra headdresses worn by the royals in ancient Egypt. Similarly, the solar descent grants us personal power through self-awareness. It enables us to discern who isn't mature enough to take responsibility for their unconscious actions so we can set boundaries with them accordingly.

This is why Ishtar, the mature version of Venus, was said to have both her warrior and lover aspects balanced. Once the queen is anchored in our psyche, we don't refrain from speaking our truth, and we have the inner strength to create endings as needed, knowing we'll return from the pain of loss and separation.

Fear of outgrowing our partner

For many years, I led women through the solar descent journey as a nine-month Inner Goddess Initiate Priestess course. Before the course commenced, I'd have a private session with each initiate, giving them a 'Goddess archetype' intuitive reading.

This process revealed which of their archetypes were the most disempowered, and therefore likely to be the most challenging for them. Without fail, every woman who was in a partnership would tell me she was afraid that taking this journey of self-discovery would result in her outgrowing her partner.

These women's fears were valid and common. This pattern is illustrated in the myth of Ishtar, who, as you learned earlier, returns from her descent journey to find she has outgrown her immature partner. She gives him the evil eye – a euphemism for naming his shadow – so he too can become self-aware. Only then can the pair enjoy a mature relationship.

Creating the inner marriage

As I explained earlier, women undertook the seven initiations to meet their chakra Goddesses to activate their Shakti as a preparation for the sacred rite of marriage. My intuitive guidance suggests that in the ancient world, women who completed the solar descent journey would commit to taking it *again*, to meet and integrate their inner masculine aspects.

This is also based on my personal experience of the solar descent. Over a number of years, I was put through it seven times before being guided to unveil my inner masculine archetypes within the seven chakras during the darker months of autumn/winter.

My intuitive understanding is that there are *two levels* inherent in the solar descent. The first is to heal and empower the seven aspects of one's foundation gender, and this is followed by a return trip to heal and empower the seven aspects of one's opposite gender – this creates wholeness within.

This is why in the myth of the Egyptian Goddess Isis, she is described as wearing both the Sun disc and the Crescent Moon horns, indicating her status as one who has descended to reclaim both her feminine and masculine aspects. Isis's quest is to restore the seven feminine and seven masculine aspects that comprise the awakened soul.

This is also illustrated in the myth in which Isis's husband, Osiris, is cut into 14 parts by his jealous brother, Seth. Isis then sets out to assemble Osiris's parts, which ensures his return from the Underworld (and hers). This process is the foundation for the seasonal descent journey of sacred union known as the *Hieros Gamos*; we'll explore this in the next chapter.

The making of a God/Goddess

The ancient Egyptians believed that what distinguished a person as a God or a Goddess was whether they had willingly descended to integrate both their feminine and masculine aspects – for it was their wholeness that made them holy. Completion of both levels of the solar descent was prized because it opened the central channel within the nervous system. (I explain this process below in the White Path of Tantra.)

Once this inner rainbow bridge of seven chakras was fully activated, the initiates possessed 'gnosis' – the ability to access divine knowledge via their intuition. This is why the Egyptians valued this process of initiation as their main form of education.[1] It is claimed that many of history's distinguished visionaries studied the teachings of the ancient Egyptian mystery schools,[2] including Pythagoras,[3] Plato and Aristotle.[4]

The White Path of Tantra

In the East, this practice of reclaiming and balancing all seven feminine and masculine aspects was called the White Path of Tantra. In addition to the archetypal teachings at the seven chakras, initiates would dedicate themselves to devotional practices that activated both the feminine and masculine energy meridians – known as 'Ida and Pingala,' the twin serpents.

These practices activated the caduceus – the alchemical symbol of healing and wholeness – within their energy field. This path is called 'Jnana' yoga (similar to Inanna yoga). Jnana means 'the path of wisdom' or 'the eight yogic practices.' The eighth practice – maithuna, or sacred sexual union – represents the awakening of the Godhead within the eighth chakra, which is situated one foot above the head.

This is why Ishtar was depicted with a halo of eight stars, and the Hindu Goddess Lakshmi was represented by an eight-pointed star mandala. Eight is the number of abundance and power, signifying one who has found these qualities within themselves.

Jnana yoga

Below are brief definitions of the eight yogic practices of Jnana.

Asanas

Physical poses that create flexibility and strength; they support the ascension of the serpent of kundalini, which expands our consciousness.

Pranayama

Cyclic breath work that balances our left-brain/right-brain function and activates our inner 'serpent of light.'

Dhyana

A meditation to focus and still our rational mind.

Mantras

Words of sacred intent and power – such as chants, affirmations, and invocations.

Yantras

Symbols used as keys to awaken codes of divinity. Specific practices include painting the chakra mandalas as a sequence to awaken one's 'serpent power' or meditating upon sacred mandalas to open specific chakras.

Mudras

Hand positions used to create specific circuitry within the energy field of our body. These stimulate the flow of energy in various meridians, activating states of greater awareness.

Bandhas

These are energy locks created through the contraction of specific muscles that distill the energy raised through a *kriya* (a cycle of yogic practice designed to activate an upward flow of kundalini through our central nervous system).

Maithuna

A sacred sexual practice that directs kundalini through intent, rhythmic breath work, creative visualization, and stimulation of the sex organs. This is combined with the ability to surrender and experience waves of deepening pleasure.

The more one can enter the chaos of the unknown, the greater the crescendo of ecstasy experienced. This is followed by an expansion of consciousness known as the 'yin orgasm – a meditative state of bliss and union with existence.

Exercise: Shakti dance

Here's an activity to help awaken your Shakti power.

❖ Put on some rhythmic music and stand with your legs hip-width apart, your knees bent. Feel your feet connecting with the ground then close your eyes and visualize sending energy roots from the base of your spine down into the center of the Earth.

❖ Next, start to move your hips in a figure of eight while breathing up red life force from the center of the Earth. Invoke your Goddess power, like the Volcanic Goddess, Pele. Allow the energy to move freely, expressing your primal fire through movement and sound to wake up your energy.

Emergence of the Shakti woman

Shakti is the energy that can move mountains. Like the Chinese proverb: 'When sleeping women wake, mountains move.'

Shakti awakens our full wattage, our primal feminine power to birth and create in accordance with our deepest truth. This is why the sacred feminine was oppressed, because Shakti is the greatest threat to any regime that seeks to dominate the populace.

The solar descent process awakens the volcanic energy of Shakti. It electrifies our light body. So when we awaken our Shakti we often experience *kriyas* – rushes of energy moving through our central nervous system or emanating from within a specific chakra. *Kriyas* often indicate a confirmation of an intuitive insight. Alternatively, they can be the release of an energetic block. The more kundalini you generate, the more *kriyas* you're likely to experience.

I was recently guided to re-enact the specific movement of a *kriya* in slow motion, immediately after I felt one rush through my field in a somatic therapy session. This gave me instant connection with the emotion needing to be released, rather than just the nervous energy. Activating our kundalini heightens our sensitivity, so I find it very helpful to take the mineral magnesium daily, as it supports the nervous system.

SUMMARY

- ❖ 'Shakti' is a bioelectrical energy current known as 'serpent power.' When activated, it awakens our Goddess essence and personal power.

- ❖ We activate our Shakti power through the seven electrical substations within our energy field known as chakras.

- ❖ When we understand and empower the seven Goddess aspects that govern the seven chakras we can enjoy a range of benefits, including longevity, vitality, increased libido, creativity, and personal empowerment.

- ❖ This path of solar descent helps us make the transition from princess to queen, giving us a foundation for mature and conscious relationships.

- ❖ Practices such as Jnana yoga are also helpful for awakening our Shakti essence.

Yin reflection time

Take a few moments to do the 'dead man's pose' – the asana for the crown chakra. Lie on the floor (or on a yoga mat) on your back (bend your legs if you need to support your back), and rest your arms by your sides. Turn your palms upward to the ceiling and close your eyes.

Allow your thoughts to drift, contemplating all that you've absorbed from this chapter.

This process is ideal after the 'Shakti dance' as the active meditation helps us to then enter the opposite polarity of stillness. By creating a space of receptivity you may receive intuitive messages or insights, or simply integrate this information on a deeper level.

Chapter 6
The Wheel of Eight

The best known of the three initiation pathways of ancient Goddess-worshipping folk is the journey around the seasonal mandala (the seasonal descent). Known as the 'Wheel of Eight' (pictured below), it has eight energetic gateways, known as Sabbats, which were observed in turn by ancient peoples as a practice to grow and mature with the seasons.

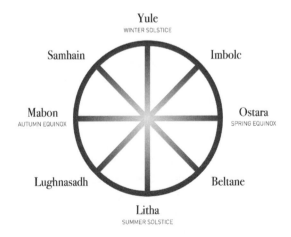

The Wheel of Eight

The eight Sabbats

The eight Sabbats in the Wheel of Eight are three-day 'power windows' revered as holy days and celebrated with festivals. They were the times when the ancients would gather and observe the lesson of each seasonal gateway, knowing this would ensure a bountiful harvest.

This timeless wisdom applies today, so if a person wants to launch a project, plant a garden, birth a child, create a mature partnership, or grow wise with the seasons, the Wheel of Eight is a template to ensure what is sown thrives into its fullest potential

The practice of observing the lesson of each seasonal gateway on the Wheel of Eight was widespread. It was known by many names, including the 'Star of Ishtar' in Mesopotamia, the 'Eight Sabbats' or 'Esbats' in Old Europe (Neolithic Europe), and the Eleusinian Mysteries in ancient Greece.

The Sabbats are the times of the year when we experience a vortex of heightened energy, catalyzed by alignments between the Sun and the Earth. As a result, they were set aside for performing sacred ceremonies with the intent of anchoring Heaven on Earth at sacred sites, the power places on the global energy grid.

From Sabbat to Sabbath

The word 'Sabbat' comes from the ancient Babylonian term 'Shapattu' ('heart rest'), which referred to the 15th day of the lunar calendar: Full Moon.[1] Judaism took this concept and created the weekly 'Sabbath' – a day of rest (from Friday to Saturday evening) marked by a family feast and religious observances.[2]

While some scholars claim the Shapattu was considered a holy day of rest to honor the menstruation of the Goddess, I suspect it was also a time devoted to the sacred sexual practice that was central to the Goddess tradition.

Why? Full Moon is the time of union between the God and Goddess. For it's when the Moon, which rules the feminine, reflects the most amount of sunlight, which is the masculine principle, creating magnetism between gender opposites.

In the Tantric traditions of Hinduism and Buddhism, Full Moon is the time of the month when male initiates invoke the sacred masculine and female initiates invoke the sacred feminine and make love with the sacred intent of harmonizing opposites for the greater good.

It's less likely for a woman to menstruate at Full Moon. However, should it have occurred, it was considered the greatest honor in the Tantric tradition for a man to lie with a menstruating woman. For this was when a woman was considered 'closest to the divine,' during her most inward phase.

However, regardless of the fluctuating rhythms of the female fertility cycle, it makes sense that this was a time dedicated to ritual lovemaking – a practice that was afforded the utmost respect by ancient Goddess-worshipping cultures.

Sacred power places

The ancients harnessed the natural vortices of the Wheel of Eight and its Sabbats by erecting ceremonial sites. These employed sacred geometry to create 'cones of power': upward spirals of energy to support the evolution of the collective consciousness. Some of the structures created for this purpose were:

❖ **Stone circles** Stone circles were sites activated through invocation during the Sabbats, serving as multidimensional portals for sacred intent. A circle has no beginning or end, so it creates a vortex conducive to raising and directing energy.

❖ **Pyramids** Researchers have recently discovered that the ancient Egyptians used sandstone containing a high degree of magnesium – a mineral that assists the raising of kundalini – in their pyramids, also designed to create a cone of power.

Furthermore, these structures were supported by foundations containing quartz crystal – a mineral that generates energy. Although long presumed to be burial chambers, the pyramids were in fact incubation chambers for healing and ceremonial work.[3]

❖ **Mounds** Mistaken by scholars as burial tombs, mounds were erected as ritual womb spaces for psychological death and rebirth. They were specifically designed so the first rays of dawn light would enter the ritual chamber of the initiate seeking a psycho-spiritual rebirth each winter solstice

The marriage of Heaven and Earth

Observing the lessons of the Wheel of Eight is a sacred tradition that grew from the Neolithic agricultural Goddess-worshipping communities, who remained humble in the knowledge that their survival depended on the perpetuation of their line (by bearing children) and the cultivation of food.

The sacred rites performed at each Sabbat ensured people remained wedded to the land: heart, mind, and soul. They were considered important to ensure the sacred balance of feminine and masculine energies necessary for the fertility and sustainability of the land and her people, so all social classes attended them; this included prisoners, who were granted temporary freedom to do so.

The Wheel of Eight consists of eight seasonal festivals (Sabbats):

❖ **Four solar festivals**: the solstices and equinoxes (see illustration above).

❖ **Four fire festivals**: the cross-quarter festivals that occur halfway between the solstices and equinoxes. Their Celtic names are Imbolc, Samhain, Lughnasadh, and Beltane. See illustration above.

Solar festivals

The solstices are the polarities of extreme light and dark that occur during the longest day in summer and shortest day in winter. They challenge us energetically, emotionally, mentally, and physically to embrace the zenith of feminine and masculine energy – internally in our psyche and externally in our relationships.

The equinoxes are the balance points that occur halfway between the solstices. They are when we experience equal day and equal night, creating a balance of light and dark/ masculine and feminine energies.

Fire festivals

The cross-quarter festivals are the halfway points between the solar festivals that mark a shift in the energies that impact our psyche and relationships. We'll explore these in more detail later in this chapter.

A man/woman for all seasons

As with most sacred mysteries, there's much speculation about what actually occurred, due to the potency of the initiations being upheld by the privacy afforded the rite. What we do know is that they consisted of a sacred cycle of ritual theater plays that included ceremonies offering audience participation. These were open to men and women, providing an opportunity for all to mature with the seasons.

Just as the solar descent was the journey of the Maiden/ Knight, the Wheel of Eight was the journey of the King/ Queen, who completed the full wheel to create conscious partnerships and accept the changing phases of parenthood. Given this book is focused on the Goddess, I'll focus on the lessons of the sacred feminine here.

Keeping the patriarchal daughter chaste and innocent

It's symbolic that in the patriarchal faerytale *Sleeping Beauty*, the king orders all the spinning wheels in his kingdom to be locked away to prevent his daughter from pricking her finger on a spindle and experiencing her inevitable loss of innocence. As a result, she falls into a sleep state in her father's domain, instead of journeying around the 'Wheel of Life' to discover the depths of the Underworld and become wise in her own right.

Without access to mentoring around the Wheel of Eight, represented by the spinning wheel, she is prevented from seeing her own shadow and experiencing sexual initiation, which would lead to her maturation. Fortunately, young audiences today are being exposed to films like *Maleficent*, *Mirror, Mirror*, and *Snow White and the Huntress*, which feature a curious Maiden who seeks to know the dark feminine in order to find her personal power.

The eight stages of the mythic journey

My understanding is that ancient festivalgoers participated in several days of ceremony for each Sabbat, eight times a year around the annual cycle. Throughout the year they would re-enact the eight stages of the mythic journey of separation and reunion, undertaken by those walking the path of relationship – be that as the holy couple or parent and child who comes of age, such as in the myth of Demeter and Persephone.

Note In 1582, Pope Gregory introduced the Gregorian calendar, and as a result, 10 days were lost, as October 5 became October 15. The dates of the solstices and equinoxes were updated to reflect this change, but the dates of the cross-quarter festivals remained the same. So the original dates still commonly celebrated are not the midway point between the solstices and equinoxes. Below are the commonly accepted dates. For times and dates that take this calendar change into account according to your time zone, visit: www.archaeoastronomy.com/2016.html

Autumn equinox (Mabon)

Northern hemisphere: September 21

Southern hemisphere: March 21

Festival of the Dying God

This is the first of the eight Sabbats, where we celebrate those willing to seek and surrender to an ego death. If a man (or a masculine-dominant woman) in a partnership is unwilling to begin this conscious descent with his beloved, the female (or feminine-dominant partner) will consciously or unconsciously give him the 'kiss of the spider woman' and show him his shadow in an effort to destroy his immature delusions. This is also where parents must let go of their children once they come of age, by blessing them to individuate and enact this cyclic journey around the Wheel of Eight.

Lesson

This equinox marks the initiation gateway of the dark Maiden – a woman who seeks her own shadow to become whole, instead of seeking to be completed by another. This is illustrated by the mythic heroine Ariadne, who enters the labyrinth to save Theseus – a symbol of her own journey to awaken her inner hero and become whole. Along the way, the Maiden meets all the aspects of herself. The first lesson of the seasonal wheel is to release what no longer serves our growth, to grieve endings, and reflect.

Samhain

Northern hemisphere: October 31

Southern hemisphere: May 1

Festival of Death

The second Sabbat is where we celebrate death as our greatest teacher. So instead of scapegoating others, we focus on seeking out our own disowned aspects. If we are wise, we invoke the unseen help of those beyond the veil, as illustrated by the Greek heroine Psyche, Vasilisa (from the Russian folktale *Baba Yaga*), and even Cinderella, who all seek help from the ancestors and the 'little people' (the fey) to navigate the dark. This Sabbat marks our last chance to release anything or anyone that's not honoring our growth.

Lesson

This is the Sabbat of the dark Mother – where we see our destructive side and face our greatest fears about ourselves and the unknown path ahead. We need to trust our intuition to guide us, one step at a time, recognize we cannot control the outcome, and relinquish any notion of control over others.

Winter solstice (Yule)

Northern hemisphere: December 21

Southern hemisphere: June 21

Festival of Conception

At the third Sabbat we celebrate the spark of life and new awareness that seeds during the darkest time of the wheel in the universal womb: the Underworld. This is when the hero/bright Maiden is reborn through facing his/her darkest fears. This is the time of the ego death, when we recognize we are too exhausted to keep fighting 'what is.' Deep in the cave of death/rebirth we experience our 'dark night of the soul' or 'shaman's death.' This is the transition phase of birth, when we beg for death in any form, to stop the torment.

Lesson

This is the Sabbat of the dark Crone – she who honors how necessary it is we express grief to completely let go of the past and our attachment to it. This is when we face the darkest truth about ourselves, which humbles us into a state of complete surrender to a higher power. This crossroads catalyzes the conception of the bright Maiden, who is reborn from the baptism of her own tears and conceived in the abyss of the void within.

The origins of Easter, Christmas, and Halloween

Ever wondered what gorging on chocolate eggs has to do with the death and the resurrection of Jesus? Well, most of our modern religious holidays have their roots in the rites celebrated by Goddess-honoring folk. For example, Easter was once Eostre, the springtime festival of birth and new beginnings, which featured a 'Moon hare' as a symbol of fertility, along with painted eggs.

Halloween was the autumnal festival that helped people acknowledge, and laugh at, their fear of death, their shadow, and the unknown. Christmas was once the silent, holy night of winter solstice, when people would gather round and decorate the evergreen tree as a symbol of enduring life during the darkest night.

Imbolc

Northern hemisphere: February 2

Southern hemisphere: August 2

Festival of New Growth

The fourth Sabbat is where we celebrate the return of the light. It's the time when we receive insight into the previous stories we held, which were the root of suffering within our psyche. It's when we start to feel a growing sense of hope as the inner Maiden strengthens with the growing light of the Sun. A new perception crystalizes within us, born from a state of humble innocence.

Lesson

This is the gateway of the bright Maiden. While we're still in our winter cave – the 'Winter of our discontent,' to quote Will Shakespeare – we've experienced a 'turning point.' So instead of basing our identity on the projections or conditioning of others, we've found our own authentic truth.

This is the birth of our independent spirit, which ushers in an urge to define our own views and opinions. This process is assisted by observing synchronicity – these coincidental observations catalyze intuitive insights that help us make sense of anything we've struggled to accept and integrate in the dark of winter.

Spring equinox (Ostara)

Northern hemisphere: March 21

Southern hemisphere: September 21

Festival of the Great Rite

This is the fifth Sabbat, where we celebrate the 'White Wedding.' It's the start of the chaste courtship in which existing couples reconnect after their time of emotional and psychological separation. It's also when new couples often meet. This chaste courtship ensures the union is built on a foundation of soul innocence – humility and transparency through the sharing of humble insights.

Lesson

This is the Sabbat of the Virgin Bride. The word 'virgin' once meant 'priestess,' a woman who was sovereign – meaning she belonged to no man. Here, we set clear intent and boundaries to honor ourselves. This is a time of exploring our own potential through planning, research, and exploring possibilities in all our creative endeavors.

Beltane

Northern hemisphere: May 1

Southern hemisphere: October 31

Festival of Fertility

This is where the lovers consummate and celebrate their nuptials and pledge to marry for a year and a day. This signifies that they will journey around the seasonal wheel again. The lovers enact the sacred sexual rites of the *Hieros Gamos*, invoking the energies of the God and Goddess through themselves as conduits, to anchor the intention of fertility for the land and her people. (This can be done within heterosexual and homosexual unions since we all have feminine and masculine energies within.)

Lesson

This is the seasonal gateway of the fertile queen. It's a time to commune with loved ones and celebrate our ability to create: whether that's a relationship, a child, or a creative project. This is when we see and enjoy the fruits of our labors. As indicated by the dance around the maypole – the decorated phallus plunged into the new green coat of the Earth Mother – we weave our creations with love around the union of Mother Earth and Father Sky.

Summer solstice (Litha)

Northern hemisphere: June 21

Southern hemisphere: December 21

Festival of the Gestating Mother

The seventh Sabbat is when we celebrate the growth that's supported through the harmonious union of opposites. Whether that's a creative project we are developing by drawing upon our inner feminine and masculine, or the gestation of a new life. Summer solstice is the longest and lightest day of the year.

Lesson

This is the gateway of the gestating mother. In the Empress Tarot card, one sees the Sun shining and a field of wheat and sunflowers depicting this time on the seasonal wheel. This is a time to invest in our own growth, and nurture the growth of our ideas, relationships, and children. These are the 'good times' that will inspire us when things get hard, so it's important to acknowledge all that is fulfilling in our lives. This is a time to shine brightly, sharing our gifts with loved ones and the greater community.

Lughnasadh

Northern hemisphere: August 2

Southern hemisphere: February 2

Festival of the Harvest

The final Sabbat celebrates all the goodness that comes through a mature attitude, such as unions and communities that invest a consistent, co-operative effort. This is a thanksgiving time on the seasonal wheel where we express gratitude for abundant crops, animals, healthy families, and communities.

This is a time to share the surplus so everyone enjoys 'the good life,' including those who are dependent on others because they are very young or very old. By working together to seed, plant, tend, and harvest, everyone has cause to celebrate.

Lesson

This is the gateway of the harvest queen – she who extends her generosity to others in service. It's the end of the summer festival season, when we turn our attention to preparing for the dark times ahead. This is a time of accepting responsibility by reviewing our harvest and being accountable for it.

Exercise: Celebrate the seasonal wheel

Try the following suggestions for embracing the lesson of each Sabbat in a spirit of celebration.

Autumn equinox (Mabon)

❖ Have a bonfire and burn a scarecrow in honor of the dying light of the Sun God.

❖ Have a day with friends making jam or sauce, and sing to enchant the brew with love.

❖ Drum around a fire – to banish any fears of surrendering to highest will.

❖ Walk a labyrinth as a meditation to go within (see Chapter 11 for more information on this Goddess symbol).

Samhain

❖ Dress up as your disowned self, such as the part of you that you judge, hide, or reject, and embrace it with humor.

❖ Laugh at your fears by speaking them one at a time in circle.

❖ On a piece of paper, write down the things that no longer serve you, then burn the paper to release them into the ether.

❖ Invite your ancestors to 'dine with you' by making their favorite recipes and sharing their stories.

Winter solstice (Yule)

❖ In circle, take it in turns to light a candle and speak what's currently challenging you.

❖ Cook a festive meal, then take it in turns to consult an oracle deck and share your lesson.

❖ Sing heartwarming sacred songs, such as Earth chants, around a fire, or share inspirational poetry.

❖ Take it in turns to humbly ask the Universe for assistance, invoking the support of the Clan Mothers or your ancestors.

Imbolc

❖ Wear white to celebrate the return of hope and innocence.

❖ Play games to lighten up after the depths of winter and invoke the magical child.

❖ Write all your new insights in a journal.

❖ Do candle magic by etching into a candle a quality to invoke for the spring.

Spring equinox (Ostara)

❖ Take vows to honor yourself, based on what you learned over the darker months.

❖ Make flower wreaths to wear or hang on your door.

❖ Create a manifestation map with a collage of images and words.

❖ State your intent for relationships.

Beltane

❖ Make posies of flowers and deliver them to your neighbors' doorsteps.

❖ Hold a garden party with a maypole.

❖ Jump the broom or fire, to pledge your love for a year and a day.

❖ Plant a love garden with your favorite flowers.

Summer solstice (Litha)

❖ Have an outdoor dinner party and decorate your table with yellow flowers to honor the Sun.

❖ Dress as faeries, a la *Midsummer Night's Dream*, and make music under the stars.

❖ Hold a bonfire night on the beach.

❖ Invite everyone to share their light with a community arts show or dance.

Lughnasadh

❖ Bake and break bread with friends.

❖ Share in circle all the things for which you're grateful.

❖ Share your garden produce and celebrate with a blessed shared feast.

❖ Create a mandala altar by making an artistic representation of the Wheel of Eight; then invite everyone to place on it something that symbolizes their harvest.

SUMMARY

❖ The Wheel of Eight is a template that ensures every stage of the life cycle is honored to ensure fertility, sustainability, and maturity.

❖ For the ancients, this practice ensured relationships matured with the seasons to support healthy families and communities.

- ❖ Ancient Goddess-worshipping cultures held sacred ceremonies at each of the seasonal Sabbats to harness the potent energy of the alignments between the Sun and the Earth; this anchored the harmonious balance of opposites.

- ❖ The festivals were enacted as sacred mystery plays that initiated participants through the lesson of each Sabbat.

Yin reflection time

Consider how this cyclic approach to relationships could address our current high divorce rates, which result in family breakdown. Now ponder how you could apply this understanding to your own relationships. And celebrate the Sabbats with your loved ones or community.

Chapter 7

Goddess phases of the lunar cycle

The third Goddess pathway of initiation is the lunar decent, or journey of the 13 Moons. As I explained in Chapter 4, it involves facing and integrating our disowned traits and behaviors at each of the 13 New Moon phases in a calendar year.

Before undertaking that practice, initiates would be taught how to embrace the lunar cycle for their wellbeing and balance. So that's what we're now going to explore. Then, in Chapter 9, we'll delve deep into secret women's business in the Red Tent or Moon Lodge – the sacred space where the lunar mysteries were held.

Let's begin with a look at the four main phases of the Moon, and how they affect the human psyche.

Welcome to the lunar mysteries

Did you know that there's a way to avoid fearing or loathing your 'time of the month'? In this chapter you'll discover how to feel like a Goddess all month round, by understanding the four Goddess 'phases' that are evoked in our psyche by the lunar cycle.

Note: If you're menopausal, please don't skip ahead, thinking this chapter doesn't apply to you. Women still cycle energetically with the lunar phases once menstruation ceases. In fact, this is when your feminine power is at its strongest...so read on!

How the lunar phases affect us

Most people are aware that the Moon's gravitational force affects the rise and fall of the ocean tides here on Earth. Considering that the average adult human body consists of 65 per cent water, it's not surprising that hospitals and police stations experience higher admissions during a Full Moon, as this is when we collectively experience a 'high tide' of emotions.

The ancients understood the Moon's effect on humans too. Paleolithic women marked their cycles in accordance with the Moon on ivory horns, sticks with 'breasts,' and eagle bones.[1] As nomads, they needed to know when their period was due and when their baby would be born, to ensure they weren't inconveniently 'between caves' at those times.

In the Neolithic era, Goddess-worshipping societies continued to create such 'lunar calendars' so they could perform communal activities in accordance with the phases of the Moon. They acknowledged the effect the Moon had on their energy levels, mood, libido, fertility, psychic abilities, and mental states.

They considered it paramount that girls understood their own connection with the lunar cycle when their menstrual cycle began. So menstruating girls were invited to attend lunar ceremonies and taught to strengthen their 'subtle senses' so they could assist the tribe with their intuitive abilities – just as we have five earthly senses, so we have five subtle ones that get stronger, like any muscle, the more we use them.

Many modern women don't understand the effect the lunar phases have on them, and feel ashamed that they sometimes feel overwhelmed and irrational. When women are not taught how to live in alignment with the lunar cycle, their contribution to society and their credibility are undermined, as women's irrational behavior defies rational explanation without a cyclic context. Fortunately, increasing numbers of women are reclaiming this cyclic awareness, and are feeling more empowered as a result.

Develop your lunar qualities

The more we develop the strengths of our lunar nature, the more we heal and empower our feminine sense of self. This is key for us as women who are healing not only our own perception and expression of the feminine, but also the collective consciousness after 5,000 years of oppression. Here are some practical tips to help you develop your lunar qualities:

1. Reflect regularly on your life experiences to develop insight and wisdom.

2. Nurture yourself and others equally.

3. Establish a sense of belonging through inclusive community-minded initiatives.

4. Act on your intuitive guidance (your first subtle impressions).

5. Honor your sensitivity instead of suppressing it.

6. Recognize your changing needs in accordance with your cycle.

7. Choose friends who are capable of giving mutual emotional support.

Exercise: A Full Moon rite to heighten your intuition

For this, you'll need a glass bottle, spring water, and a moonstone crystal. (If you don't have a Moon diary or calendar, you can find the date of the next Full Moon at: www.timeanddate.com/moon/phases)

❖ On the night before the Full Moon, pour the water into the glass bottle and insert the moonstone crystal. Leave the bottle outside, to bathe in the Moon's light.

❖ On the night of the Full Moon, stand with your arms raised and see yourself as a crystal chalice drawing down the luminescence and blessings of Great Grandmother Moon. This is ideally done outside, but it doesn't have to be.

❖ Fill yourself up and visualize your third eye (the energy center located between your brows) glowing with the light of the Full Moon. Then anoint yourself with the Moon elixir in your bottle, vowing to honor your intuition by always acting upon it.

❖ Finally, fill a goblet with your Moon elixir, and bless the gift of intuition distilled within its alchemical structure. Toast the celestial

Clan Mothers (the ancestral wise women), thanking them for watching over you and guiding you.

Why women fluctuate like the Moon

Have you ever wondered why women are so changeable? From our fluctuating weight to all the moods we traverse in any given week, we have greater highs and lows than our male counterparts. Why is this? It's because the lunar cycle governs the feminine psyche and hormonal cycle, and the Moon fluctuates a lot more than the Sun.

For example, the Moon changes astrological signs every two and a half days, whereas the Sun changes signs once a month. The Moon has four main phases within a 28-day cycle, whereas the Sun experiences four equivalent phases within a 365-day solar year. So while for us as women it can be personally challenging to experience so much change, it's an opportunity to accelerate our psycho-emotional growth.

How do we do this? By consciously seeking to understand how the lunar phases and transits through the zodiac signs are affecting us. For example, as the Moon moves from one sign to the next, we feel the influence of each sign, regardless of our personal horoscope. When the Moon waxes and wanes through its four main phases – New Moon, First Quarter Moon, Full Moon, and Last Quarter Moon – this also influences us. There isn't room here to explain the effect of the Moon in all 12 zodiac signs, but you can follow my lunar blog for daily updates via www.themoonwoman. com

Simply by being aware of the lunar phases, we can apply their lessons and experience less emotional drama.

The four main lunar phases

Here's a brief overview of the four main phases of the Moon, along with tips for thriving in each one.

New Moon

In this phase, the Moon isn't visible to us at night because the Sun and the Moon are conjunct (appearing on top of one another). During this phase we're more likely to feel tired, inwardly focused, and vulnerable. This is the monthly crossroads when we can experience a psychological death and rebirth if we contemplate the beliefs and conditions that we've outgrown.

This is a time when our psychic senses are amplified, making it ideal for meditation, conscious manifestation, channeling, and women's sharing circles. If your fertility cycle has ceased, this is the time of your 'energetic period.' It's also when the majority of women menstruate. (This is the deepest and most challenging time of the month, when initiates who undertook the path of the 13 Moons would observe the lessons being evoked by the New Moon transiting through each zodiac sign in turn.)

First Quarter Moon

One week after New Moon, the Moon appears half-illuminated. This is because it forms a 90-degree angle to the Earth and the Sun. During this phase, we're likely to take risks, have more energy to exercise, and feel more social. This is a great time for putting ourselves 'out there' by sharing ideas, launching new projects, or planning social events. This is a time of doing, rather than reflecting.

Full Moon

This is the third week of the lunar month, when the Moon is most visible and luminous. Why? It's aligned with the Earth and the Sun, but is on the opposite side of the Sun, so it reflects more sunlight. Full Moon is when we often experience the culmination of either our conscious intent or the unconscious expectations that we seeded at New Moon.

Emotions tend to run high now, and it can be a challenge to stay energetically grounded and get to sleep. This is the ideal time to celebrate life with a party or a shared meal, as we can weather late nights more easily. There's also an innate urge to indulge our feminine desires for connection, communion, and sensual pleasure.

Recent scientific evidence suggests that sleeping with exposure to the Full Moon regulates menstruation. This is because lunar wattage resets our endocrine function.

Last Quarter Moon

In the final week of the lunar cycle we tend to feel increasingly inward and contemplative as the light of the feminine diminishes. It's best to conserve our energy as much as possible during this week – if we commit to too many social activities, we may find we don't have the energy to attend them. This is the ideal time to have some early nights, and catch up on journaling, reading, and quality solitude.

The Goddess phases of the lunar phases

Each of the four main Moon phases evokes one of the four Goddess phases we journey through in our life cycle. The more familiar we become with the qualities and strengths of each Goddess phase, the more we can embody them with assurance and grace.

New Moon: the Crone phase

At this time of the month, the archetypal wise woman comes to the fore. This is the Crone Goddess: 'she who sees everything.' If consciously embraced, the Crone helps distill our power by taking our awareness deep within for intuitive insight, leaving a legacy of wisdom for others to follow.

First Quarter Moon: the Maiden phase

In this phase, the Maiden Goddess – 'she who experiences the return of hope and inspiration' – takes up residence. If consciously embraced, the Maiden gives us an air of light-heartedness, and belief in the pursuit of our dreams.

Full Moon: the Mother phase

The Mother Goddess is the dominant aspect during this phase. If consciously embraced, 'she who is full of the milk of human kindness' helps us to nurture ourselves and encourage others to fulfill their potential.

Last Quarter Moon: the Enchantress phase

During this phase we experience 'she who is sovereign, mature, and responsible for her harvest in life.' The influence of the Enchantress phase helps us integrate our life lessons to ensure our choices reflect our core values.

The Goddess phases of our fertility cycle

Each phase of our monthly fertility cycle also evokes one of the Goddess phases within our psyche. While these often coincide with their respective Moon phases, numerous factors can affect this, so don't worry if they're not in sync. For example, after a big life change our cycle will often shift, so we bleed with the Full Moon. When this happens, our psyche is indicating we're not open to procreating or merging with another. So our body refrains from sending out enticing ovulation pheromones at Full Moon – which is party time!

Similarly, many girls begin their menstrual cycle around Full Moon so their descent into the deepest parts of their psyche isn't as intense as it is at New Moon. So trust your body, she knows exactly what she's doing!

Here are the Goddess phases evoked by each fertility phase:

Pre-ovulation: the Maiden (First Quarter Moon)

This is a time of blossoming like a flower – the symbol of the Maiden who feels filled with potential. This sense of youthful spontaneity and ambition is felt whether we're 18 or 48! Our behavior can be impetuous so it's important we consider the consequences of our actions, and don't over-commit due to our sense of limitless possibilities.

Ovulation: the Mother (Full Moon)

This is our fruiting stage, when we're at our most fertile. Not surprisingly, more babies are born at Full Moon. This is when we have more energy, so we're more loving, kind, and patient. We're also more open to communication and our scent is more enticing, indicating we're full of feminine energy and more inclined toward physical intimacy.

Post-ovulation: the Enchantress (Last Quarter Moon)

This is the ripening stage when the strength of our essence intensifies, like a semidried fruit or fine wine. As our energy starts to wane, we become discerning about how and with whom we spend our time. This results in clearer boundaries and an urge to spend time alone, or with those who have developed their feminine sensibilities.

Menstruation: the Crone (New Moon)

We return deep within now – like the seed that contains all – due to the 'Moon flow' spiraling in our womb. This takes our consciousness deep within: into a meditative state. We may look pale and drawn, due to the loss of our life force. We often become aware of that which must be released in our lives – along with the release of our uterine lining and unfertilized egg.

The diagram below illustrates the Goddess phases of the fertility cycle.

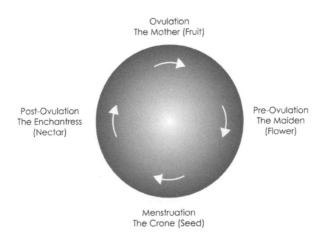

Ovulation
The Mother (Fruit)

Post-Ovulation
The Enchantress
(Nectar)

Pre-Ovulation
The Maiden
(Flower)

Menstruation
The Crone (Seed)

Exercise: Color your moods

For one month, record the 'color' of your mood at each of the four main
lunar phases. To do this, go to www.timeanddate.com/moon/phases/ to
find the dates of the Moon phases; next, draw a circle and divide it into
four parts – one for each phase. Then, every week, choose a color that
best illustrates your feeling, energy levels, and mindset at each phase.
You may also wish to mark where you are in your fertility cycle for each
phase. For example, menstruating, or two weeks later, ovulating.

Analysis time!

Compare the results for both the lunar phase and your fertility phase
to review the effect of these influences. If your cycle is in sync with the
Moon, your highs and lows will be more pronounced.

This process is designed to illustrate why we don't feel like smiling every
day. In having this awareness we don't place unrealistic expectations on
ourselves to be bright and sunny every day of the month.

SUMMARY

* The main Moon phases evoke the four Goddess phases we journey through in our life cycle.

* The four phases of our monthly fertility cycle also evoke these four Goddess phases within our psyche; if these cycles coincide, we experience greater mood swings.

* When we understand each Goddess phase, we can better attend to our needs to enhance our emotional balance and energy levels. This reduces addictive behaviors like comfort eating.

* By being aware of both the lunar phases and the lunar transits, we can better caretake our needs.

Yin reflection time

Cast your mind back to your relationship with the Moon as a young child. Did you talk or sing to the Moon? Did you feel as if she had special powers? Consider doing some 'Moon bathing' to bask in her healing, feminine light. Simply lie under the light of the Moon and breathe in her luminescent energy; Full Moon is the ideal phase to do this.

Chapter 8
Rites of passage

Now that we've explored the Goddess phases evoked by the lunar and fertility cycles, we're going to examine how they play out in our life cycle. In ancient Goddess-worshipping communities, women were assisted through their transitions into each life stage with mentoring, and ceremonies that helped them embrace each Goddess phase.

These practices are known as 'rites of passage,' signifying the sacred rites (rituals) and teachings that were a woman's birthright. The good news for us is that, once we too receive guidance and initiation into our own rites of passage, we cope much better with periods of change and the inevitable aging process. So what follows is Goddess guidance for each stage of your feminine journey.

The feminine fear of aging

It's no great secret that we live in an age-phobic society. This fear is projected more on women, due to the patriarchal culture that values women primarily for their use to men as lovers and mothers. However, there's another reason why many women struggle with the aging process – fear of chaos and the unknown.

Our cultural obsession with youthfulness reflects how disconnected most people are from the feminine perspective that everything in life is cyclic, including us. Ironically, if we surrender to the inevitable circle of life, we spend less time worrying about aging, and the result is a more carefree and youthful outlook on life and fewer worry lines.

Whereas if we resist nature and employ all manner of artificial means to reverse the clock, we end up looking more like a caricature of an earlier life stage, rather than an authentic version of our current one.

For women, surrendering to the cycle of life is easier said than done. We're constantly exposed to marketing campaigns that target our insecurities – implying that our natural process is unacceptable to society. I'm referring here to the cosmetic ads in which women wear the white lab coats of scientific authority and tell us to 'fight the feminine signs of aging.'

This sort of intimidation only works on women who are disconnected from the true feminine. Why? Because those who have access to the teachings of the sacred feminine learn to see and appreciate the gifts, strengths, and lessons in every stage of the feminine journey.

Each life stage is equal, but different. Without this understanding, women cling to their previous life stage, reluctant to move on for fear of the unknown. The lack of awareness about our need for rites of passage results in unnecessary stress, due to inadequate mentoring and support. Consequently, women embody the shadow traits of their current life stage and fear the aging process.

Exercise: Review your life goals

This process will help you to really embrace your current life stage.

1. On a sheet of paper, write down all the aspirations you had when you were 13. Don't hold anything back, even if it feels slightly embarrassing.

2. If you're older than 23, now write down the aspirations you had 10 years ago. If you're younger, go to the next step.

3. Next, write down the aspirations you have for your life now.

Analysis time!

Read the first list, then the second, and compare how they differ from the third one. The results indicate how much your priorities, values, and goals have changed over time. This check-in with ourselves at each major life transition helps us avoid psychological crises based on outmoded thinking and life goals.

Navigating our life transitions

In order to embrace the transition phases in our life journey, and help our daughters through theirs, we need to identify their lessons. Let's look at the threshold into each stage of our feminine journey by exploring its lesson and identifying the correspondences that illustrate the energy of each phase.

Threshold of the Maiden

The official start of our maidenhood is when we start cycling with the Moon with the onset of our first menses. This auspicious occasion is called menarche (pronounced men-ar-key). It is when we often experience our first loss of innocence.

Without adequate preparation for this internal identity shift, girls can feel uncomfortable with their changing body and unready for the responsibility of fertility. While necessary, science lessons discussing reproduction, or 'safe sex' talks, don't help a girl address the inner swings she feels between needing security and seeking independence.

Maiden phase correspondences

- ❖ Color: white
- ❖ Element: air
- ❖ Season: spring
- ❖ Direction: the east, the place of the dawn
- ❖ Focus of intent: expressing the Self
- ❖ Blood rite: menarche

Maiden phase lessons

Explore our potential and individuate: In order to individuate successfully from our mother, we must learn to be responsible. If we don't earn trust through being accountable, we may rebel, or never find the courage to pursue our independence. In this phase we need freedoms equal to our responsibilities. If our responsibilities aren't honored, we ought to lose our freedoms until we can demonstrate accountability.

We need affirmation of our strengths and potential, and encouragement to pursue our goals – using our natural gifts to make a difference. This helps counteract feelings of overwhelm as we become aware of the collective shadow (everything that seems wrong with the world).

Navigate the shadowlands: Every month as we approach our bleeding time, we experience darker thoughts and feelings that need to be understood and integrated. If we're taught to understand this natural process, we trust that we'll resurface after each menstruation with greater understanding. This awareness enables us to embrace our 'down time' as an opportunity to become more self-aware. Without this understanding, we may fear being eclipsed by our darker moods or act destructively, causing harm to ourselves or others.

Threshold of the Mother

A woman does not need to have given birth to enter the Mother phase. Although if she has given birth, this transition will demand that her psyche makes the shift from Maiden to Mother, regardless of her age. The threshold of the Mother is known as the 'death of the Maiden.' It requires us to renounce our independence and modify our external goals to consider the needs of others and make appropriate compromises.

This also happens for us when we marry or cohabit with a partner, or, to a lesser degree, when we adopt a pet. Given that for modern women, the preparation for birth consists only of hospital visits and buying baby clothes, it's not surprising that many experience postpartum depression. They have no guidance or initiation ceremony to anchor the psychological ego death that parenthood demands.

Mother phase correspondences

- ❖ Color: red
- ❖ Element: fire
- ❖ Season: summer
- ❖ Direction: the place of midday (south in the Northern hemisphere and north in the Southern hemisphere)
- ❖ Focus of intent: birthing/nurturing
- ❖ Blood rite: birth

Mother phase lessons

Share and co-create sustainably with our opposite: As in the saying 'The bigger they are, the harder they fall,' the more independent and ambitious we are, the more challenging this transition is. For, in order to create and sustain life, we need to learn the art of cooperation.

Research shows that relationship conflict escalates after the birth of a baby, as parents struggle with the increased responsibility and workload.[1] If there is mutual respect for the respective roles of nurturer/provider, together the couple can weather the storm. However, if both parents are not equally committed and mature, one will eventually resent parenting the other, and withdraw their attention on the partnership to focus on the child.

Nurture the Self in order to sustain giving: The degree to which we can identify our own needs – and make meeting them a priority – is the degree to which we can sustain tending to others' needs. To do this, we need to recognize that our needs as women are cyclic. It's important that mothers, especially sole parents, take time out to tend to their own needs around New Moon – the darkest time of the month for the feminine psyche.

Without this awareness, women lash out at their kids, or implode into depression, which erodes their confidence in their ability to mother. Similarly, if we get into the habit of staying up late after our kids are in bed – to 'have some headspace' or 'get things done' – we'll eventually hit the point of complete exhaustion, since children wake early and require supervision and care.

Threshold of the Enchantress

This is when we enter our second maidenhood – our forties and fifties – indicated by the second (waning) Crescent Moon in the lunar cycle. This is a time when those in our care assert more independence, so we have more time and space to consider who we are and what we want.

It's also when many women really make their mark in life and make a difference – using their time and talents to create a better world. Unlike the earlier Maiden phase, we're less likely to suppress our voice in order to win external approval. We know ourselves, so we have the inner power and experiential wisdom to really make an impact. This is when we make adjustments to create a life that reflects our deepest values – inspiring those who walk in our footsteps.

Enchantress phase correspondences

❖ Color: maroon

❖ Element: water

❖ Season: autumn

❖ Direction: the west, place of the sunset

❖ Focus of intent: reflecting/healing

❖ Blood rite: perimenopause

Enchantress phase lessons

Heal past wounds and develop self-trust: We can often experience what appears to be a setback – such as illness, divorce, job loss, or loss of a loved one – at this threshold. Such experiences act as catalysts for developing resilience, inner strength, and trust in ourselves, so we can overcome what we perceive as obstacles.

External challenges facilitate a confrontation with our vulnerability. This requires us to stop and acknowledge the impact of our past, and take responsibility for healing the parts of us that still carry wounds. This can be a time of facing our fears in order to realize our greatest strengths.

Reclaim our personal power by expressing our authentic truth: The more we prioritize our relationship with ourselves as the foundation for all our relationships and experiences, the more we take time for self-enquiry. This self-awareness results in inner empowerment – so our external life becomes a reflection of our deepest core truth and values.

We then become aware of our ability to truly make a difference; we walk our talk in the choices we make and the actions we take. This is a time when many women discover the healing power of sisterhood, which encourages them to make the changes needed to live an authentic life.

Threshold of the Crone

The cessation of our fertility cycle indicates a shift in our focus from the external, material world to our inner, spiritual world. This is when our psychic gifts become more pronounced. If we haven't developed a conscious framework to reference our subtle perceptions, we may interpret our psychic impressions as signs we're going mad, and unconsciously direct our will to shut down our third eye.

Blocked energy at this threshold can create a susceptibility to dementia.[2] To cope with the inevitable decay of our body, we need to expand our consciousness so we can gracefully accept our fragility with the dignity of an elder.

This perspective also helps us consciously navigate our fear of death and the unknown. So the more we develop our direct connection with existence, the easier this transition and life phase becomes. At this time, our life force continues to diminish, so we become highly discerning about sharing our legacy of experiential wisdom – choosing those who demonstrate they are humble and receptive enough to receive it.

Crone phase correspondences
- ❖ Color: black
- ❖ Element: earth

- ❖ Season: winter
- ❖ Direction: the place of midnight (north in the Northern hemisphere and south in the Southern hemisphere)
- ❖ Focus of intent: releasing/gestating
- ❖ Blood rite: menopause

Crone phase lessons

Focus on self-actualization in preparation for rebirth: Death and birth are the same transition, depending on which side you stand. So the challenge here is to process everything we've journeyed until we've made our peace with every choice and experience.

This ensures we have no unresolved karma to keep us Earth-bound, or repeat in another incarnation. The fewer regrets we have, the easier it is to slip out of our mortal coil and adventure into the unknown, fully present in each moment.

Return to innocence through reclaiming the magical child within: Elders often delight in spending time with the very young. This is for a number of reasons: it gives them a sense of connection to the great cycle, a feeling of genuine contribution to an ongoing legacy, and an opportunity to simply embody the presence of love.

Spending time with those at the beginning of their life cycle also helps us to have trust in the eternal wheel of life and death. Young children are also receptive to the unseen world and embody trust in the divine plan. To interact with those who operate in a consciousness of complete unity is the most profound healing for our own wounded child. The more we enter into their world, in the inner realms, the less emphasis we place on the external one.

Now let's play a quick game...

Exercise: Cleaning out Pandora's box

Without overthinking or editing yourself, write down the names of three women in each of the Goddess phase 'categories' below. These can be women in your own life, global icons, or even fictional characters.

Maiden _____

Mother _____

Enchantress _____

Crone _____

I developed this exercise in workshops to reveal the power of acknowledging the feminine role models stored within our psyche – those that we consciously or unconsciously compare ourselves to as a yardstick.

Analysis time!

The Goddess phase categories you found easy to complete – coming up with many names – are those that you know well. Whereas the phases for which you struggled to find examples are those where you lack clear role models and may lack empowerment. Refer to the previous chapter to empower these phases during their corresponding Moon phase.

You may also wish to consider whether the women who first came to mind in each category exemplify the positive or negative traits you associate with each phase. Also consider the significance of having a higher proportion of women whom you know personally, compared with those with a public profile, or fictional characters.

This ratio can indicate an absence of strong female role models in our immediate vicinity, which leads us to compensate by piecing together icons from the collective consciousness. I recommend journaling to make more connections from the pearls of wisdom discovered in your treasure chest!

Goddess parables for each transition

The Goddess has survived through the ages in folk songs, nursery rhymes, faerytales, children's games, and holiday traditions – sometimes knowingly, but often not. So when we discover that all these seemingly unrelated customs are in fact part of a tapestry woven by our mothers, grandmothers, aunts, teachers, and neighbors, we start to realize the Goddess was with us all along – we just hadn't been formally introduced.

The myths of ancient Greece and Rome were the descendants of fables held sacred and re-enacted as community rituals by earlier Goddess-worshipping cultures. Oral storytelling was highly regarded in the Goddess tradition, and parables were revered as teaching tools to shape minds and cultural values and heal the psyche. They were especially useful in assisting people of all ages to transition through their life stages.

What follows is an overview of three such 'medicine stories' for the life transitions of Maiden, Mother, and Crone.

Maiden phase (menarche) myths

The first transition in the feminine cycle is menarche, and in fact, many of the faerytales we grow up with are distorted 'menarche myths.' As a result, girls do not associate their coming of age with happiness; instead, they have an unconscious expectation that it will be fraught with danger and marked by a lack of support from their feminine role models.

Consider three of the most popular faerytales of the patriarchal era: *Sleeping Beauty*, *Cinderella*, and *Snow White*. In *Sleeping Beauty*, a princess is cursed by a magical woman at her birth and on her 16th birthday; in *Cinderella*, a girl is bullied by both her stepsisters and her stepmother; and in *Snow White*, a stepmother hires a hitman to destroy the heroine, only to later tempt her with a poisoned apple.

These stories are symbolic of the way women's wisdom was poisoned. When the folk tales previously shared via the oral tradition were written down, twists were added in order to disempower the feminine. But, before you burn all the Disney princess outfits in your daughter's wardrobe, take a moment to pause...

If we hope to heal our feminine lineages we can't expect to stem the tide of popular culture. What we *can* do is start a conversation that questions and discusses the lessons highlighted by the stories we share with our girls.

Similarly, it's wise not to assume that our girls are 'too old for stories.' For it's often the faerytales they most loved as children that become ingrained and symbolic in their feminine journey. For example, *Little Red Riding Hood* reminds girls in their teens and twenties – who are entering the shadowlands – where they'll make their greatest mistakes. It shows them the lessons they'll encounter, so let's look at this story.

Little Red Riding Hood

We meet Red Riding Hood, a young girl, on the first day that she's trusted to leave the safety of her mother's house and enter the woods alone. Her mission is to visit her grandmother, who is unwell, and deliver some home-cooked food.

On the way, Red Riding Hood meets a wolf who attempts to exploit her naïvety in various ways. First he extracts the details of her route, intent, and destination. Then he tries to seduce her off her path with the idea of picking flowers for her grandmother (he intends to beat her to the house and devour her there). Finally, he dresses as Red Riding Hood's grandma and tries to entice the girl to come close enough to be dessert.

Teaching: This tale illustrates the feminine cycles: as the archetypal wise woman is waning, her granddaughter is blooming. Red Riding Hood sets out on the path to her grandmother's house, symbolizing her journey to become a wise woman in her own right. She's exploring her independence, afforded her by her red hood – a symbol of feminine fertility (this indicates that she's begun her cycles). To become wise, she must learn to navigate the dark, and discern friend from foe, by attuning to her intuition (her inner knowing).

Red Riding Hood's first test is to assess whether the wolf has earned enough trust for her to share her private information. The second test is whether to allow a potential predator to distract her from her path. The wolf's invitation to pick flowers is a euphemism for plucking the flower of her virginity.

Some versions of the story include a third test, in which the wolf appears dressed as a sheep, indicating a man who will shapeshift into whatever form he thinks she desires, rather than reveal his true nature. Her final test is to identify and name the predator for what he is – a wolf.

Red Riding Hood's empowerment is found in acknowledging the truth to herself and others, as well as using her intuition to discern truth from falsehood and friend from foe. This is the feminine way of self-defense: using one's wits instead of brute force.

In the patriarchal version of the story, Red Riding Hood is saved by a woodcutter who sets her free from the belly of the beast. This implies that some men who hear the call of the wise woman will defend and champion the sacred feminine, while others, who are not civilized, will seek to deceive and devour her sexually.

Exercise: Once upon a time

In a journal, write your personal story as a faerytale. Next, consider which childhood folktale it most closely resembles. Then write a new ending for your story in which you emerge as a self-empowered Goddess.

Mother phase myths

The second life transition in the feminine cycle is our sexual awakening. This second phase of individuation from the mother can be challenging if a daughter chooses a partner her mother doesn't approve of. Especially if the mother fears the partner might harm her daughter. Ultimately, we can't prevent our daughters from experiencing the shadow side of life, as it's part of their 'getting of wisdom.'

What both mother and daughter *can* do is acquaint themselves with the universal teachings offered by Goddess parables. The increased awareness of both parent and child helps ease tensions, which can build through both parties feeling misunderstood.

In ancient Goddess cultures, young women were prepared for marriage by the elder women in the community, who would tell stories that illustrate the cyclic nature of relationships, such as the one that follows. This tale depicts the transitions that occur, for both mother and daughter, when the daughter experiences her sexual awakening.

The descent of Demeter and Persephone

Demeter, the Mother Goddess of Grain and Agriculture, once lived on Earth with her daughter, Kore, whose name means 'pure maiden.'

One day, Kore plucked a narcissus flower, which caused the Earth to open and take her into its depths. During her time there, Kore resisted all temptations, except six ruby red seeds from a pomegranate. Having eaten these seeds, she made the transition from virgin – 'a woman unto herself' –

to Persephone, the wife of Hades (the mythic ruler of the Underworld during the patriarchal era).

This meant Kore was unable to return to life as an innocent child with her mother. From this time on, she was bound by the great cycles, spending six months of each year in the darkness of the Underworld and six months in the fertile lands of her mother.

Teaching for the daughter: Kore makes the inevitable shift from being the product of her mother's influence to a queen in her own right, with her own clear identity – evidenced by her name change to Persephone. She does this by 'tasting her own dark fruits' in the roots of the Tree of Life. She sees the darker side of herself and others, marked by the exploration of her carnal nature.

This is symbolized by Hades offering her an exotic new fruit, a pomegranate, as an alternative experience to the apples offered by her mother. In the ancient world, sharing pomegranate seeds signified entering into the covenant of marriage.

It's interesting to note that when girls become sexually active, many undergo an outer transformation that signals their change of feminine identity. Instead of sporting 'Pollyanna'-style hairdos and clean-cut clothes, they experiment with more seductive attire. This archetypal transformation was iconically portrayed in the musical *Grease*, when squeaky-clean Sandy showed up strutting her new bad girl image in black tight pants, and with wild hair and red lips – which are symbolic of a blood-engorged vulva.

Teaching for the mother: In the story, Demeter makes the transition from having her daughter as the center of her world to recognizing she must release her control and focus on her own process. Her challenge is to trust in the foundational values she's instilled in her daughter, knowing she will inevitably explore the opposite of everything she has taught her.

The degree to which Demeter suffers during the individuation of her daughter is directly dependent on how connected she is with cyclic lore. In the patriarchal version of the myth, Demeter's grief is compounded by the betrayal of her daughter's father, Zeus, who consents to Kore's abduction by his brother, Hades. Whereas in the earlier matriarchal version, Demeter willingly surrenders Kore, recognizing she is sexually curious and that her carnal desires will result in her making decisions that aren't always wise but inevitable in her getting of wisdom.

During her period of grief as she integrates this life change, Demeter lacks the energy required to tend her crops, resulting in a barren wasteland. This signals that even in the Mother phase we must honor the cycles that govern us, and attend to our inner process in order for new growth to occur. The key is, the more we accept change, the less we struggle with the process. The second half of the Demeter myth, in which she faces her aloneness, constitutes the lesson of the Enchantress phase.

Crone phase (menopause) myths

As discussed earlier, many women fear aging, but this is not just down to vanity. In a patriarchal culture, an elder woman is regarded as having no value. The following tale of the archetypal wise woman, or Crone, once echoed around the world in numerous cultures. It teaches the true value of one who had journeyed all the life cycles.

Myth of Hel, Goddess of the Underworld

In the ancient Norse tradition there was a prophecy about three unusual children who would bring about terrible suffering. So when the demigod Loki mated with the giantess Angraboda, their offspring came under suspicion.[3] Their firstborn was a wolf, their second-born a serpent, and their third, Hel, had exposed bones on half her body. Hel was so-called because the name meant 'one who hides.'[4]

The children's uncle, the God Odin, decided it was best to keep them close, so he brought them to his kingdom of Asgard. Life was very difficult for Hel in Asgard as her appearance meant everyone avoided her. Eventually she asked Odin if she could leave Asgard and he agreed, appointing her guardian of the Underworld.[5]

The Underworld then wasn't considered a place of punishment: it was the womb cauldron of the Great Mother where heroes descended for psychological rebirth. Hel's role was to act as a guide, by drawing on her own experience of suffering. The most famous of these heroes was Baldr, whose brother came in search of him. Hel refused Baldr permission to return to the Upper world, until all who knew him had expressed their grief.

Teaching: Hel shows us how everything we experience eventually becomes our greatest offering to others. As we age, those who are focused on the external world pay us less attention. As what they've not yet traversed holds little interest, or is frightening, for these people, so they distance themselves to avoid facing their fears of death and the unknown.

Those who are excluded for being socially unacceptable revert more to exploring the inner realms. This means they're not afraid of being in the dark, for they have seen the darker side of human nature and learned to process their own fears. Hel learns the value of suffering and grief. She knows firsthand that if we don't express the landscape of darker thoughts and feelings, we will be lost in limbo, neither fully alive nor dead. Only by honoring our feeling nature can we awaken the wise woman.

Exercise: The seven signs of aging

Take a moment to contemplate all the ways that your life has improved as you've aged. Then write down seven positive traits you've developed with age.

This process reveals how we develop the real gold within as our soul matures, making the quality of our life richer.

SUMMARY

❖ To age gracefully, and embrace each life stage, we need to take time to review our past chapters, including our values and goals. We can then update them and avoid comparing ourselves with outmoded ideals.

❖   The more empowered our feminine sense of Self, the more easily we can cope with change.

❖   The theme in our Maiden phase is to explore our potential and individuate.

❖   The theme in our Mother phase is to find a balance between the needs of Self and other, union and separation, giving and receiving.

❖   The theme in our Crone phase is to explore our inner world so we can be in alignment with our external world.

Yin time for reflection

Allow yourself 15 minutes to gaze out a window at the sky, look upon your garden, or stare into a fire and allow your mind to wander. Notice the impressions this chapter has made on your psyche. Are you left with feelings of sadness or hope? What are the memories that underpin those feelings? Which of the life phases held the greatest number of insights for you, helping you to reframe and embrace it?

Chapter 9

Secret women's business

In this chapter we'll explore an ancient tradition that's enjoying a resurgence around the world today: the Red Tent (also known as the Moon Lodge) – a sacred space in which women gather 'in circle' once a month to connect with their authentic truth by acknowledging, expressing, and sharing their deepest thoughts and feelings.

The Red Tent, or menstrual hut, emerged in the Goddess-worshipping matriarchal communities of Neolithic times, when women menstruated in unison due to their shared living quarters. Young women were taught about all aspects of their womanhood in the Red Tent, including the mystical function of their 'Moon time' (menstruation), which was revered as a time for rest and renewal.

(So, contrary to the expectations put on us by ads peddling menstrual products, we're not abnormal if we don't feel like skipping along the ocean shore wearing a white bikini when we have our period.)

The tradition of the Red Tent was lost over time due to the rise of empires like Rome, which outlawed all nature-worshipping practices on the grounds they were blasphemous. But today more and more women are reclaiming the tradition of gathering and sharing in the Red Tent.

The taboo of menstruation

The word 'taboo' comes from the Polynesian word *tapua*, which means both 'sacred' and 'menstruation.'[1] Similarly, the word 'regal,' meaning 'royal power to rule,' comes from the Latin *regula*, which means both 'measure' and 'menstruation.' The word 'ritual' comes from the Sanskrit word *r'tu*, meaning 'menstrual magic.'[2]

Put that all together and it's easy to see that originally, royal power was attributed to women, who were revered for their sacred power as menstrual shamans. This is why in the matriarchal cultures of the ancient world, women were afforded time apart from their civic and family duties when menstruating: so they could cultivate their sacred power.

Over time, this tradition was eschewed. Religious patriarchs forbade menstruating women from attending their religious services, and men were advised not to engage in sexual intercourse with a menstruating woman, for fear of their psychic power.

As I explained earlier, in the Tantric tradition it was considered a great honor to lie with a woman when she was bleeding. Conversely, even today, some orthodox patriarchal religions consider menstruating women too 'impure' to prepare food. This is a stigma that the women affected would understandably not invest energy in fighting, as it means they get a rest when they're physically drained.

The sacred circle of life

Traditionally, women squatted on hay while menstruating in the Red Tent, and the hay was then used as a natural fertilizer on their crops. As agriculture shifted from a sacred practice that honored our communion with the cycles to a secular one of commercial trade, this way of 'returning the sacred blood to the Earth' was replaced with 'blood and bone' fertilizer that used ground animal remains.

Despite the conditioning that teaches women to view menstruation as dirty, and treat their blood as toxic waste, more and more women are finding ways to return their sacred blood to the Earth. They are doing this by using cloth pads or latex menstrual cups, so they can make a cyclic offering that's nutrient rich and able to support new life. If you would like to do this yourself, simply soak cloth pads in water (using a ratio of 10:1 water to blood) and then use the water as a natural liquid fertilizer for your plants. If using a menstrual cup, simply pour the blood into water and then pour on your plants.

This is a healthy alternative for both the land and our bodies, especially when we consider that feminine hygiene products containing chlorine bleach have been proven to increase our risk of cancer.[3] And that synthetic tampons and sanitary pads containing pesticides and dangerous chemicals like BPA and BPS – which disrupt embryonic development – continue to be sold to unsuspecting women.[4]

The Grandmother Lodge

In the Native American tradition, women who reached 'Moon pause' (menopause) were said to have attained their feminine power.[5] This is because the trance state we enter into during our bleeding time is seen as practice for our elder woman phase – when we walk between the worlds due to our expanded psychic sensitivity.

For this reason a separate sanctuary, called the Grandmother Lodge, was available to the elder women to use as needed. It was a great honor to be invited to sit with the elder women in this lodge. Every woman who had crossed the threshold of Moon pause was considered a grandmother, regardless of whether she had borne children. These women continued to be welcomed and honored at the Red Tent and were revered for the collective wisdom they accumulated there.[6]

Welcome to the Red Tent

In Goddess-worshipping cultures, a girl was welcomed to sit with the women in the Red Tent when she began cycling with the Moon, as indicated by her first period. Most modern women are not offered this initiation to their womanhood, but fortunately, it's never too late for us to receive it – even if we no longer menstruate.

Receiving this initiation rite in the form of a creative visualization will anchor in you the precious nature of your womanhood, which in turn will inform your choices as a woman. I recommend finding somewhere private, quiet, and comfortable to sit as you read the section below, taking your time to connect with the words and visualize the imagery.

Take yourself back to when you started your periods. Now see your mum presenting you with a beautiful red dress and moonstone earrings that have been passed down from her mother and her mother before her. Next, she draws you a bath with sweet-smelling oils and red rose petals, and leaves you alone with music that takes you into a trance state.

You emerge from your bath feeling clean and soft. You put on your ritual dress and earrings, and your mother then takes you to the 'Red Tent.' This is where the women gather for 'Secret Women's Business' and you've been curious to know what that entails. Tonight you will find out.

The building is domed and made of mud brick. There are beautiful stained-glass windows. Inside is a foyer in the shape of a Crescent Moon with Goddess paintings, wall hangings, and statues of the Goddess in all her phases. You experience a sense of expectancy as you hear the low, rhythmic sound of hoop drums emanating from the central chamber.

Your mother parts sheer red curtains and ushers you inside a beautiful temple space. The air is scented with incense, lit candles are all around, and there's a central altar decorated with a mandala of flowers, crystals, and candles. All the women who have known you throughout your life are there – your grandmothers, your aunts, your godmother, your mum's friends, the mothers of your closest friends, and your neighbors. They are all gathered to welcome you to your womanhood. Close your eyes and see yourself receiving this blessing.

Honoring our ability to feel

Gaining access to this sacred initiation rite can act like a key, unlocking a deep remembrance in our souls of something once considered special and honored. This can evoke a complex array of feelings, including joy that we've finally received this gift, grief that we didn't receive it earlier, and despondency when we consider the difference it may have had on our self-image and choices.

In my experience, it's not unusual for women to grieve when they finally receive this long overdue welcome to their womanhood. So if your heart needs to grieve, please let it. As stated in the previous chapter, grief is an appropriate response that helps us to process our past. Grief allows our heart to soften, so we don't compensate with a shield of righteous indignation and anger.

Allowing ourselves to connect with, and express, deep feelings like grief enables us to access greater states of joy. If we deny an emotion, it blocks our full spectrum of feeling – and our true strength as women lies in our ability to feel.

Transforming pain into wisdom

Sharing our feelings with others can seem alien or scary if we aren't comfortable with them. Understandably, many women shut down their feeling nature in an effort to cope in a culture that devalues feelings and perceives them as a sign of weakness.

However, it's through connection with our feelings that we develop self-awareness, heightened perceptions, and greater connection with others. These are the qualities that help us cope in life. And it's through our feelings that we connect with our deepest truth and innate wisdom: our greatest strengths.

The women's sharing circles facilitated in sacred temple spaces like the Red Tent/Moon Lodge enable us to practice attuning to our heart's truth and express our authentic feelings. This helps us remain receptive, with an open heart, instead of becoming hard in an effort to protect our vulnerability. And when we're centered in our heart we find it easier to respond to life's challenges intuitively from our heart's wisdom – like being calm in the eye of the storm during a hurricane.

If women don't have a safe space in which to connect with and express their feelings, they tend to retell their latest drama from the perspective of their 'mind' in a social setting – such as complaining over coffee and cake. This can heighten the drama and induce greater levels of stress. This is because 'social space' evokes the ego (personality) whereas 'sacred space' evokes the soul – the part of us that's transparent and vulnerable but wise.

Sharing circles enable women to respond to their life challenges with greater grace and dignity. They do this by providing sisterly support dedicated to helping women identify and master their personal lessons. This is one of the reasons why the Red Tent was pivotal in indigenous cultures; and it's why it's resurfacing today as a global phenomenon.

A mystic perspective on 'women's problems'

In addition to improving our mental and emotional wellbeing, the Red Tent supports our physical wellbeing. 'Women's problems' is a term clinicians use to refer to female reproductive health issues. These are centered in the sacral chakra – the energy center that governs our emotional body. If women don't regularly express their emotions, chronic illness results in the organs governed by this chakra.

Without an understanding of the way the Moon influences our psycho-emotional states, or access to a regular women's sharing circle to support them during the lowest phase of the Moon, many women feel powerless in the face of stress and chronic health issues.

And, in addition to the accumulated stress we experience when we're oblivious to the ways of honoring our feminine sensibilities, there's the collective stress we inherit through our ancestral lineages. The more sensitive we are, the more likely it is we'll also be affected by the shared collective pain of our sisters, due to the cultural denial of all things feminine.

But today, more and more women are finding that having a supportive space where they can process their life challenges, reduces their stress levels and improves their wellbeing. And in turn, this minimizes chronic health conditions.

The more connected women are through our shared lunar rhythms, the more empathy we have for each other. And as more of us experience a homecoming to sacred women's traditions, and shed tears of joy and grief, we help heal the collective. In this way, we lighten the load and enhance the wellbeing of *every* woman on the planet.

The power of the Red Tent

When women gather in the Red Tent with the intention of sharing their thoughts, feelings, and experiences in a sharing circle, they dignify them by allowing their full expression – unlike in a social space, where one tries to preserve a social mask. In circle, each woman is supported to speak in turn, without interruption. A skilled group facilitator midwifes the psycho-emotional death and rebirth process as needed, encouraging each woman to connect with the full depth of her feeling.

By fully inhabiting our feelings, we move through them and birth a new, empowering perspective. We need to feel held and supported on all levels in order to surrender to our feelings. This is the true power of circle. Women who don't have access to this regular form of support during the darkest phase of the lunar cycle are at risk of depression, self-harm, or destructive patterns of behavior. Women who regularly attend Rent Tent circles are able to clear blocked emotion, which helps access their intuition.

In the ancient Goddess cultures of North America, if you wanted to destroy a village you simply destroyed its heart, its place of wisdom: the Red Tent. So the fastest way to rebuild our global village is to reclaim our heart wisdom by reinstating the tradition of the Red Tent.

Wisdom is developed through reflecting on our life lessons, and this was one of the main functions of the Red Tent. It was there that women were encouraged to embrace their spiral descent journeys by acknowledging their darker thoughts and feelings, in order to gain insight from their unresolved experiences.

During the patriarchy people were taught to fear the cyclic descents into their darker thoughts and feelings as a one-way ticket to eternal suffering in 'Hell' – a word appropriated from 'Hel,' the Norse Goddess we met in Chapter 8. In matriarchal times, the Underworld was considered the great womb of rebirth. It was understood that we all descend there periodically to gestate and birth a new identity and awareness.

The Underworld is an inner state into which we descend when we bleed. The more we understand this, the more we can embrace our need for a safe space to rebirth ourselves by experiencing an inner shift from breakdown to breakthrough.

Indigenous peoples understood that when women gather, their 'womb power' is amplified – this is, their ability to create through intention. This is why women were revered for the healing work they would do for the collective in the Red Tent through sacred ceremony, meditation, and healing practices.

Then and now, the Red Tent also provides women with a physical womb space in which they feel supported to descend into an internal womb space. It's a maternal place of nurturance, acceptance, and authenticity.

Creating a womb space

For years I traveled to women's homes to conduct rites of passage ceremonies. This involved creating 'pop up' Red Tents in their living rooms using red fabrics, velvet cushions, Persian carpets, candles, and peacock feathers. Afterward, most women didn't want me to remove the Goddess 'makeover' of their home, because the resulting 'womb space' was so nurturing, feminine, and inviting.

You may like to create a womb space for you and your daughters, if you have any, in which you can nurture your periodic feminine need for rest and reflection. For example, when my daughter received her first period, she sat in my bed and we drew around her the red tulle canopy above it, so she was sitting in a mini Red Tent. You may like to create a red room with a cosy fire, candles, and lots of books, or decorate a children's tipi with faery lights and red cushions.

The sharing circle

While other activities happen in the Red Tent (see below), the central practice is the sharing circle. This is what catalyzes deep personal transformation for everyone who gathers with the intent of acknowledging their shadow – their innermost secrets, self-criticisms, vulnerabilities, and shame. While it's easy to love the parts of ourselves that feel socially acceptable, it's much harder to love those parts we're deeply ashamed of.

The Red Tent is where we support each other to face our dark side and be accountable for it. This process enables us to integrate the disparate parts of our psyche, so we feel self-aware and empowered through greater self-acceptance. This is called 'shadow work,' and it's why the Red Tent is held during the dark Moon phase – the three days before, during, and after the exact time of the New Moon.

Those who don't have a regular practice for owning their shadow, project it onto others, which can create conflict in relationships. The more we, as women, learn to appreciate the role of the dark Goddess in our own lives, the more our partners will revere, rather than reject, this aspect within us.

Speaking, witnessing, and honoring truth

The strength of the sharing circle is its ability to hold our deepest truth with reverence. So, to ensure a safe 'container,' whatever is shared in circle 'stays in circle' – this honors each person's privacy.

A talking stick (a sacred object usually used only for circle, such as a clay Goddess statuette or a serpentine-shaped tree branch), a scarf, or a bowl is passed around, indicating each person's right to speak, one at a time, from the heart and without interruption. Adhering to these guidelines enables us to:

1. Connect with our authentic truth, through connecting with our feelings.

2. Be truly seen and heard, which is deeply healing (see box below).

3. Feel held energetically and emotionally if we experience emotion.

4. Review the previous month by reflecting on our experiences and lessons.

5. Process our past experiences so we're resolved to start the new lunar cycle.

6. Learn from the collective and develop compassion and sisterly love.

The gift of being seen

I recently booked a healing session in order to address one of my core wounds: the perception that I'd been a burden to my father. I'd observed that this belief had led me to compensate by choosing male partners who were a burden to *me*, just so I wouldn't feel the pain of being a burden to a man.

During the session I regressed back to being a toddler, and the pain I felt in my heart was a response to perceiving my father's lack of delight in me. It felt as if he couldn't comprehend my light, or reflect it back. So, instead of us experiencing shared moments of joy, I felt diminished – like a Sun imploding in my heart.

When the session facilitator asked me to take myself to a time when I'd experienced others greeting me with pure delight, I found myself in my Red Tent circle. I can't put into words how healing it has been to be truly seen, heard, understood, appreciated, respected, affirmed, and validated. That's what inspires me to deliver this gift to every sister on the planet!

The benefits of the Red Tent

Compassion fatigue is inevitable for us as women, since we hold everyone else – emotionally and psychologically. By having a regular window to discharge pent-up tension, we can sustain our role as nurturers. I remember hearing of a mother at my daughter's primary school who'd committed suicide. It pained me to think that outcome could've been averted if she'd had a Red Tent sisterhood.

In the Red Tents I facilitated, women did not want to leave! They'd quenched their thirst for their most primal need –

to belong – in a space where they could dare to show all of themselves, without fear of being excluded for being unacceptable.

It's this authentic sisterhood that heals the wounds of our experience of being targeted by the 'shadow feminine' – such as immature 'mean girls' of all ages who compare, gossip, judge, compete, or exclude other women, often in subtle and manipulative ways. Inclusion is the way of the sacred feminine – that's the healing power of circle as a practice.

Other Red Tent customs

In addition to helping women honor their inner 'dark Goddess' during their death phase each month, the Red Tent fulfills a very important role in the community. It's where women gather to learn and practice their feminine gifts. Here are some of the other customs practiced in the Red Tent, both traditionally and today.

Storytelling

Parables are shared that reveal life lessons and help us grow our feminine wisdom through understanding archetypal lessons (see Chapter 8).

Dream and symbol analysis

We share and interpret the messages given to us in the form of dreams and symbols.

Healing arts

We harness our expanded sensory perception during dark Moon/menstruation by practicing and sharing our healing modalities. Among these are herbal lore, energetic healing techniques, and soul midwifery for birth and death.

Meditation

Since dark Moon is the easiest time to enter the stillness within, we practice being receptive, and meditate on our highest intent for our community.

Sacred crafts

What became known as 'domestic crafts' were once revered for creating objects of sacred power. Therefore, we learn skills such as basket-weaving, pottery, and baking.

Divination

Oracles are consulted for guidance, and divination arts are practiced. Traditionally, these included casting the bones (interpreting scattered animal bones), scrying (gazing into a dish of water or a black mirror for visions), reading tea leaves (to discern symbols), and Tarot cards – all of which strengthen our insight and intuition.

Manifestation

After reviewing our life lessons and releasing our burdens, the exact time of the New Moon is used to seed our intent for the coming month.

Mentoring

We exchange practical advice to help each other with our daily tasks, and meet the challenges of child-rearing.

Sacred ceremony

The Red Tent/Moon Lodge holds the accumulated sacred power of all our past ceremonies, making it a powerful space for performing ceremonies to assist an individual or the collective.

Rites of passage

The Red Tent is where we prepare for all our feminine rites of passage and celebrate them with initiation ceremonies.

Channeling

Our ability to intuit and channel information is increased when we gather with intent, so the women of the village were once revered for the guidance they accessed for the greater community during their time in the Red Tent.

Sacred sexuality

Young women are privy to open conversations about sex and marriage, so they aren't unprepared for their first sexual encounter. Women are taught to honor the sacredness of their bodies, and traditionally were taught which native plants to use for contraception or to enhance fertility.

Temple dance

The power of the womb is taught through the sacred art of belly dance, which tones the uterus with the aid of an inserted jade egg. This practice helps women to physically prepare for and recover from childbirth.

Yoni steaming

Dressed in a long shift and without undergarments, we take it in turns to sit on a birthing stool and let the steam from a pot of boiling water infused with herbs placed beneath us, tone, cleanse, and heal our intimate temple space. This practice was performed by women in the Mayan culture of Central America, whereas African women would burn sandalwood and use its sacred smoke for the same purpose; they would do it prior to marriage and then once a month thereafter.

Blood magic

Women are taught to revere the magical and regenerative properties of their sacred 'Moon blood' by using it to consecrate ritual tools and healing amulets. The sacred blood is also used as a libation in sacred ceremony and poured on magical and medicinal herbs, to encode them with sacred feminine wisdom and healing.

Note: Please be assured that if you attend a public Red Tent women's circle, the chances of being invited to steam your yoni, insert a jade egg or paint amulets with your menses is about 1:10000000001.

This level of shared sacred work is engaged in by women with an intimate sisterhood bond, developed over time within a private Red Tent circle. Public circles usually involve a sharing circle and introductory processes. So, if you'd like to go deeper, consider starting your own private Red Tent circle with your closest girlfriends. I offer training online if you'd like to learn to facilitate a Red Tent circle; visit themoonwoman.com

Sacred beauty

Rather than spending a fortune at a spa, we exchange pampering treatments such as hair-braiding and waxing during our time in the Red Tent. Since touch is the most primal form of love, we feel nurtured through the loving touch of sisterhood.

The transformative power of ritual bathing

In north Africa and Turkey, women once went to the hammam (steam room/bathhouse) after their period, to exfoliate and bathe. This was done to complete the cleansing cycle of the womb, which releases the uterine lining during menstruation. By skin-shedding inside and out, women felt reborn and ready to embrace their new lunar month.

Conversely, in Orthodox Judaism, a sacred bath known as the 'Mikvah' was necessary for women to 'become pure' before lying with their husband after their Moon time. This illustrates how the same bathing ritual can be either a source of shame or a source of healing, depending on the meaning attributed to it. By reclaiming our sacred traditions and their inherent meaning, we possess the power to heal any subconscious shame we've come to associate with all aspects of our feminine nature and identity.

There's a thermal hot spring a 90-minute drive from my home. One of its features is a Turkish-style hammam with a domed roof, a central marble slab, and sinks with hand-painted tiles and decorative silver dishes you can fill and use for rinsing. When the place first opened, I was fortunate enough to meet a Turkish woman who explained the ritual bathing practice she'd grown up doing with the women in her motherland. After they finished their Moon time, the women would go to the hammam for a ritual body scrub.

I usually visit the hammam with my soul sisters and take along handmade pumice and lemongrass soap made by my friend Sunni. We take it in turns to lie on the central marble slab, lather each other up, and then scrub away the past. With many hands nurturing us simultaneously, the simple act of washing, when done with sacred intent and sisterly love, becomes transcendent and transformative.

I've done this bathing rite with women on my Goddess retreats, and they found it bonding to experience such sacred touch among sisters. The day before writing this chapter, I went to the hot spring on the last day of the lunar month (and my Moon time) with a friend and six kids aged between seven and 15 (it was the school holidays). Still keen to experience the renewal of the hammam, I invited the kids to take part.

It felt special to teach the children of my friend how to gift their mum this simple act of love. Even the son, who has autism and can be volatile, washed his mother with the care and consideration of a licensed therapist. Later that evening, the youngest boy, aged seven, came over and gave me a hug. I knew this was his gratitude for the moments we'd experienced in the hammam.

Exercise: DIY sacred bathing

Consider how you can re-create this act of ritual bathing with your daughters or girlfriends every New Moon, with your beloved at Full Moon, or to pamper a pregnant or sick friend. If you don't have access to a steam room, consider a bed or a foot bath, or try a natural water source (just be sure to use biodegradable soap).

SUMMARY

❖ Menstruation was once revered for its sacred power. It was understood that it helped women to deepen their insight and wisdom.

❖ The way we're welcomed to our womanhood has an impact on how much we value ourselves as women, and the choices we make.

❖ Sharing circles enable us to connect with our feelings, which identify our needs, so we can respond with right action.

❖ Our collective grief at the diminishment of the feminine is a contributory factor in the high number of women who suffer from womb-related illnesses.

❖ The Red Tent provides a safe space for women to acknowledge their unconscious thoughts and behaviors, so they don't project them on others.

❖ Sharing circles held at dark Moon provide women with an opportunity to review and process the previous month.

Yin reflection time

How are you feeling? Take your awareness into your womb. What's stirring within you? Sense the effect the information in this chapter is having within your body. Is there any tension? If so, breathe into it, and release on a sigh, allowing yourself to feel.

You may wish to integrate the repercussions of this information into your psyche by going for a walk, having a bath, writing a poem, or sitting in the stillness. Alternatively, you may wish to wrap yourself in a blanket and sit in a dark room. Be soft, allow your thoughts to wander, and then record your insights in a journal.

Chapter 10

Goddess rituals and sacred ceremonies

Let's now explore the role and function of ceremony and ritual in the Goddess tradition – interchangeable terms for a sacred magical practice that's increasingly being reclaimed by men and women today. As I said earlier, in the Goddess tradition we're taught to respect the power of ritual magic – which is simply using our ability to consciously raise and direct energy through the sacred geometric power of a circle. (More on this below.)

In this chapter, we'll take a look at the ways ritual serves our psychological growth, and understand the importance of practicing ritual magic ethically. You'll also learn which events are observed with ritual in the Goddess tradition, how Goddess rituals and ceremonies are performed, and how to hold your own.

Reclaiming our human rites

The word 'ritual' can conjure up dark associations, thanks to the projections of Hollywood and the tragic abuses done to children in religious cults and secret societies. These distortions are the result of the oppression of our original 'human rites.'

Rituals are a primal human need. They are the physical acts we create to mark and integrate change. This is why we need a funeral to grieve, a divorce for closure of an intimate partnership, or a birthday party to celebrate the milestones of our children.

If we don't have access to constructive rituals during our search for meaning and belonging, we unconsciously create destructive rituals, such as:

- ❖ Hurtful pranks played on new students and employees.
- ❖ College fraternities that pressure male members to drink yard glasses and commit date rape.
- ❖ The committing of unlawful acts in order to join a street gang.
- ❖ Cheerleading squads that require new members to eat human excrement (footage seen on Oprah!)
- ❖ Brides and grooms publicly humiliated by strippers before their wedding day.

A loss of connection with our authentic ancestral rites has seen them distorted into commercial holidays that are void of true meaning. As a result, for many, life has also lost its meaning.

Fortunately, as the Goddess rises in the hearts of increasing numbers of people, we're restoring the sacred traditions that fulfill something very deep within our souls. This reconnects us with our ancestors, who performed rituals to celebrate the natural cycles of the Sun, the Moon and the seasons, and their own life stages, before the oppressive rule of the empires stamped them out.

When we gather in circle for sacred intent we amplify our power to create. The circle is therefore a very powerful tool for reclaiming our sacred sovereignty in a world hijacked by corrupt private interests and corporate greed. Fortunately, we're now seeing ritual magic positively portrayed, thanks to books such as the *Harry Potter* series and *The Lord of the Rings* and their associated movies.

Right use of power

Before we venture further into the practice of ritual magic in Goddess ceremonies, it's essential to understand the law of reciprocity (more commonly known as the law of cause and effect, or karma). This is one of the Universal Laws that were recorded by Hermes Trismegistus, a high priest and scribe who taught in the ancient Egyptian mystery schools at a time when Egyptian culture held the Goddess in high esteem.

The Universal Laws outline the energetic truths that govern existence. They appear in both Buddhist and Christian sacred texts and informed Babylonian astrology and Greek philosophy.[1] All the collated wisdom of the ancient world, including both esoteric and exoteric sciences, was held at the Alexandria library in Egypt, which held half a million scrolls and was a center for spiritual study; it was later burned by the Romans.[2]

The law of reciprocity

In the Wiccan tradition of magic (see box below), the law of reciprocity is often called the law of threefold. This states that whatever we send out comes back – with three times the amount of force. However, many believe this 'rule of three' is not literal but instead refers to the fact that the consequences will increase until the 'lesson' is learned.

Basically, it teaches us not to abuse our power by creating ill will toward a person, or asserting our influence over them. As I used to tell the four-year-olds for whom I hosted faery parties, 'If you wish for someone to trip over a chair, you'll trip over three chairs.' So it doesn't pay to use ritual magic for anything but good.

Abusing one's power is neither honorable nor wise, as any attempt to distort divine will is destined to backfire. As the faeries say, 'Be careful what you wish for' and the Bible says, 'Do unto others as you would have them do unto you.' To ensure no harm is done unintentionally, those who practice ritual magic in an ethical way always include the tenet 'In accordance with highest will and for the highest good of all' in the conclusion of any ritual intent. Stating this is like an insurance policy, placing a protective clause over anything that's said. So if it doesn't serve the divine plan, it's rendered null and void.

A brief history of modern magic

Wicca is a neo-pagan spiritual tradition that worships both the God and Goddess. It emerged in England at the turn of the 20th century in private circle gatherings known as covens. In the 1970s it spread to become a recognized worldwide religion, due to the publication of various books.[3]

It's interesting to note that originally, the word 'pagan' simply meant 'country dweller,' although it now refers to those who worship nature. The term 'neo-pagan' refers to those from the 20th century onward who have practiced nature-based worship – honoring the natural cycles and elements that incorporate Goddess worship.

This resurgence of the alchemical traditions practiced by earlier Goddess-worshipping cultures followed on the heels of the Theosophical Society, founded in the US in the late 1800s, which also studied and practiced occult (meaning 'hidden sacred knowledge') teachings and practices.

The elements of sacred ceremony

Goddess ceremonies and rituals are not lavish affairs – they are simple, but rich in meaning. To create your own, either alone or with friends or family, follow the steps in the basic template below, which can be used for all Goddess ceremonies, regardless of their intent (purpose). Not all ceremonies are held in the Red Tent, some are held outside and include men – see step 1, below.

1. Create a ritual space

Many Goddess-honoring people like to conduct sacred ceremonies outside, to connect with and harness directly the elemental forces of nature. For example, on a beach under the Full Moon, in a garden around a fire pit, or in a purpose-built, semi-permanent circular shelter, such as a Mongolian yurt or tipi, which helps spiral the energy upward.

Once you've selected a location for your sacred ceremony, either inside or outside, create a central altar containing sacred objects that symbolize your intent. These can be symbols that signify the God and Goddess, such as a statue or image of the horned God/Green Man known as Cernunnos in the Celtic tradition (who represents the archetypal nature God) and an image of one of the seven Goddess aspects (see Chapter 5).

Alternatively, a mortar/bowl or cauldron can be used to signify the receptive sacred womb/yoni of the Goddess, and a pestle/athame (ritual knife) or wand used to signify the fertile, sacred phallus of the God. These are placed on the altar to symbolize union, on the understanding of the law of gender/duality, which acknowledges that all of creation is birthed through the union of these opposite energy polarities.

However, if the ceremony is specifically intended to invoke the powers of the sacred feminine, as practiced by female-only covens in the Dianic tradition, only Goddess representations would be used.

Many people also like to create altars to honor each of the five directions and their corresponding elements (see step 4). Round tablecloths spread on the ground make great altar cloths to designate the ritual working space. A sacred circle can also be cast using stones, crystals, shells, or flower petals, or if you're on the beach, it can be drawn in the sand. Below are some suggestions for sacred objects to honor the five elements.

- ❖ East: Air – feathers, dried white sage, or a feather quill.

- ❖ North: Fire – a red candle, a tea light candle in a red glass holder, or incense.

- ❖ West: Water – a goblet of wine or a dish of blessed water.

- ❖ South: Earth – a dish of salt, crystals, stones, or flowers.

- ❖ Center: Spirit – a white candle, white feather wings, or a selenite crystal.

Note: the guide above is for those living in the Northern hemisphere. If you live in the Southern hemisphere, place Fire in the North and Earth in the South, to honor the natural flow of energy directed by the poles.

2. Cleanse your ritual space

It's customary to cleanse one's energy field and ritual space before sacred ceremony. This can be done as people enter the circle by:

- ❖ Smudging – make a 'smudge stick' by binding together a handful of dried sage, gum, lavender, or sweet cedar leaves with yarn. Burn the top of the stick in a small earthenware dish or a shell, or hold it, and then use a feather or your hand to fan the smoke through your energy field.

- ❖ Flicking salt water with your hand or with a sprig of freshly picked herbs such as rosemary.

- ❖ Spraying an auric spray containing essential oils and vibrational essences. An auric spray is a water spray that contains blessed rain or spring water and is infused with healing symbols and intentions to cleanse one's energy field. Vibrational essences are healing elixirs that distill the energetic healing properties of flowers, shells, or crystals.

❖ Visualizing the violet flame of transmutation spiraling through everyone and the space. The violet flame is said to emit the frequency of the color ray of healing that corresponds to the crown chakra – located in the top of the head as a portal to the Divine Source. Aligning with this vibration through intent and visualization helps us integrate the lessons of the lower energy centers (chakras) and transmute lower frequencies.

❖ Using sacred sound, such as that created by ceremonial drums or rattles, blowing a conch shell, or vocal toning. These were used traditionally to clear and raise energetic space and invoke ancestral spirits and guides for sacred ceremony.

Ancient priests and priestesses in the Goddess tradition used vocal toning to clear energy and open energetic portals in ceremony. Tones are created when we modulate from one open vowel sound to another, and allow the voice to sit between the diphthong – a term used to describe two vowel sounds within a single syllable.

3. Casting circle

The purpose of this stage is to define the parameters of the ritual space. This helps contain the energy, so it builds and can be directed upward in a spiral, creating a positive vortex. This is an opportunity to use your creativity. Examples include:

❖ Passing a thread of cord around the circle as each person states his or her name.

❖ Using crystals or flowers to mark out a circle on the ground.

❖ Passing a kiss or hug of welcome around the circle.

❖ Lighting each person's candle from a central candle.

4. Invoke the elements and spirits

Next, call in the names of beloved spirits – be they your spirit guides, animal totems, ancestors, archangels, or specific Goddess aspects. These spirit allies will often make themselves known to you through synchronicity, or repetitive visions in meditation, or trance states such as those accessed through dance or rhythmic breath work.

Invite the spirits' energy as a supportive, benevolent presence by saying their name in a spoken invitation to the rite, or by naming what it is you'd like their assistance with. For example: 'I call upon the Goddess Hecate to be present and help me access insight during this crossroads.' Invoking high-frequency benevolent beings helps ensure strong, energetic boundaries and supports the positive intent being anchored through stated intention.

The next step is to harness the five elements of creation: Air, Earth, Water, Fire, and Spirit. This is done by invoking by name each of the directions that correspond to the five elements, as you turn to face them. We always start in the East, which is the place of sunrise, symbolizing new beginnings.

Note: In some group ceremonies, only the high priestess/ priest presiding over the rite will speak and face each of the directions. However, I've observed that the most powerful ceremonies are those where every person actively participates. For example, by turning to face each direction, or by toning, or by raising their arms to invoke the power of each element while visualizing themselves embodying each element in turn, following the path of the Sun.

Below are examples of an invocation for each of the directions that correspond to the five elements. They are written for either the solo practitioner or ceremonial priestess/priest to speak.

❖ **Face the East:** 'We open the portal to the East and welcome in the element of Air to inspire new beginnings with higher thought.'

❖ **Face the South:** 'We open the portal to the South and welcome in the element of Fire to create new conditions that reflect the true desires of our eternal flame.'

❖ **Face the West:** 'We open the portal to the West and welcome in the element of Water to deepen our receptivity to our subtle perceptions and compassion for all.'

❖ **Face the North:** 'We open the portal to the North and welcome in the element of Earth to ground our intent with practical support.'

❖ **Face the Center:** 'We open the portal to the fifth element, Spirit – the element of surprise! May we serve highest will through surrendering to the divine in all things.'

Note: If you live in the Southern hemisphere, you must invoke North after the East for Fire, then Water in the West and Earth in the South, due to the opposite trajectory of the Earth's gravitational spin.

5. Set intent

Once you've created an energetic container for the rite, the next step is to set your sacred intent for the rite. I like to first state a personal intent, to ensure I'm energetically centered. To do this, I state out loud, or telepathically: 'I now call back my personal energy from wherever it has been placed,' and then visualize it returning to me as particles of energy strengthening my personal energy field.

I then state out loud the intent for the ceremony itself. For example: 'We are gathered here today to celebrate the joining of Benjamin and Delphine in the rite of sacred union/holy matrimony.' The intent for the ceremony may be set by the high priestess or priest, or alternatively, by each person in turn stating their personal intent for the rite around the circle. This is ideal for Earth healing ceremonies.

6. Raise power

The next stage is to charge your intent by raising a 'cone of fire.' This is the name given to the positive vortex of energy we create through unifying the group energy in circle, while focusing on the intent. To do this, choose from one of these options:

❖ Join hands and breathe in unison while visualizing your shared intent.

- ❖ Utter an incantation – this is a spoken affirmation which, when constantly repeated, anchors your intent over and over again. This process takes one into a light trance state. Here's an example of an incantation: 'May love prevail on a global scale.'

- ❖ Sing a chant – an incantation that's sung rather than spoken. The simpler the chant, the easier it is for ceremony participants to pick up and join in and sing from their heart, connecting to the meaning of what they're intending. You can create your own simple chants or access one from the numerous examples on You Tube or online music services.

- ❖ Dance around a fire – this can also be combined with an incantation or a chant.

- ❖ If practicing alone or with a partner, you may also harness the power of self-pleasure or lovemaking to build your 'cone of fire.' As you climax, visualize your sacred intention as manifest.

In a group ritual, you'll find that the energy naturally builds until it reaches a peak, at which point everyone may dance, cheer, clap, and raise their arms to release the energy up in surrender.

7. Close the circle

Next, the elemental energies are closed down, in reverse order. This undoes the energy web that was woven for the ceremony, so participants aren't energetically bonded to one another once the rite is complete.

Below is an example of how to close the circle. Again, these invocations are spoken by the ceremonial leader or solo practitioner and affirmed by the ceremony participants, who might say 'Blessed Be' or 'So it is' at the end of each spoken command.

- ❖ **Face the Center:** 'Thanks be to Spirit for co-creating with us in our sacred circle.'

- ❖ **Face the North:** 'We close down the portal to the North. Thanks to the North and the element of Earth!'

- ❖ **Face the West:** 'We close down the portal to the West. Thanks to the West and the element of Water!'

- ❖ **Face the South:** 'We close down the portal to the South. Thanks to the South and the element of Fire!'

- ❖ **Face the East:** 'We close down the portal to the East. Thanks to the East and the element of Air!'

- ❖ **Face the Center:** 'We say thanks to all our unseen friends. Merry meet and merry meet again!'

8. Grounding

Finally, I recommend inviting everyone to place his or her forehead on the ground, to send any excess energy raised down into the Earth. This ensures no participant drives home in an ungrounded state, or gets a headache after the ceremony. It's also customary to break bread and cakes and share wine or tea to help everyone ground and celebrate the completion of the rite.

Sorcery versus pantomime

While there are books on the market containing prescribed rituals that describe exactly what to say and when to say it during ceremony, I thoroughly recommend using your own words of power – spoken from the heart and in the moment – rather than reading from a script.

Why? Your heart energy is far more potent. This is true sorcery: attuning your energy to the Divine Source and then trusting Spirit to work through you spontaneously, in the moment, by following your intuition. Although theater grew out of ritual, you don't want your ritual to be reduced to a rehearsed pantomime!

Celebrations in the Goddess tradition

As discussed earlier, the Goddess tradition honors the cycles of nature which, when harnessed, promote growth – such as Full Moon, New Moon, and the Wheel of Eight seasonal festivals – or the transitions in our life cycle. We covered the Wheel of Eight in Chapter 6, so below is a brief outline of ways to honor the New Moon and Full Moon, and the life stages of the triple-phase Goddess.

Rites of passage

When marking life transitions, the elements of sacred ceremony shown above are adapted to include an opportunity for the initiate to publicly acknowledge what they have learned and what they wish to release or call in for their next life stage. This often includes a ritual act to help the initiate symbolically release their old identity, and embrace the new one, as they cross the threshold into their next chapter.

According to American author and poet Judy Grahn, in her book *Blood, Bread and Roses: How Menstruation Created the World*, 'Anthropologists like Jane C. Goodale and Margaret Mead reported detailed menarchal ceremonies that were connected to weddings and to training young women in sacred lore, weaving, cooking, and caring for their families and communities.'[4]

Then and now, those who honor the Goddess tradition celebrate the turning of the wheel in their feminine journey by acknowledging the three sacred blood mystery rites.

Note: perimenopause isn't considered a blood rite, and therefore the Enchantress phase is not included below in the suggestions for celebrating rites of passage. However, I still recommend marking the occasion. In my experience as a ceremonial priestess hosting rites of passage, I've found many women benefit from a ceremony to embrace this phase, since it represents our second maidenhood.

You may wish to celebrate turning forty – the milestone birthday synonymous with the onset of the Enchantress phase – with a night of sisterhood celebrations after a formal women's circle and ceremony. I marked my fortieth birthday with a girl's night that included 'Kaftans, Cocktails, and Karaoke!'

Celebratory activities for rites of passage
Below are some suggestions for marking these transition phases in a woman's life:

For the Maiden

- Host a special Red Tent women's sharing circle to welcome your daughter to her womanhood.

- Draw your daughter a sacred bath with rose petals after she finishes her first period.

- Have a high tea with your daughter and take it in turns to share your favorite things about being a woman.

- Give your daughter an heirloom gift to acknowledge how special it is that she has become a woman.

For the Mother

- Use henna to paint the belly of the mum-to-be with sacred symbols and blessings.

- Have a circle and each pledge one way you'll support her after baby arrives.

- Invite the mum-to-be to write down all her fears about motherhood, then burn and release them.

- Create a birth tree of phone numbers to activate a prayer vigil once the labor begins. To do this, each female friend of the mum-to-be has one phone number to call when the labor begins; this signals that it's time to light a candle and invoke support on all levels for the birth.

For the Crone

- Invite family and friends to take it in turns to share the wisdom she has bestowed on them.

- Acknowledge everything she has helped to grow in her Mother years, and present her with a bouquet of gratitude – such as flowers and a book that records her legacy (containing written contributions from everyone who knows her).

✦ Make a crown for her, to acknowledge her status as an elder of the community.

✦ Invite her to speak about the most important lessons she learned from each stage of her journey.

Moon rites

In the Goddess tradition, it's usually only the polarities of New Moon and Full Moon that are celebrated with ritual or a community celebration, rather than every lunar phase.

Celebratory activities for the Moon rites

Below are some suggestions to mark these phases:

New Moon

✦ Find your nearest Red Tent/Moon Lodge/women's circle, where a facilitator will guide you through a process to acknowledge the shadow trait that's surfacing. (See Resources section for Red Tent directories.)

✦ Write down a clear intent for the coming month and place it under your pillow. In this way, your subconscious can manifest it while you sleep.

✦ Consult an oracle for insight – such as pulling a card from an oracle deck or a divination rune from a pouch – then ponder the meaning of the card/rune. Lastly, read the interpretation provided.

❖ Have a ritual bath – one created with sacred intent within a sacred space. To do this, put on some transcendent music, light candles, add vibrational essences, oils, and herbs/mineral salts or flower petals to the water and allow yourself to feel and release any unexpressed emotion. Meditate or utilize the elements of ceremony above to create a cone of fire to activate your intent.

Full Moon

❖ Have a shared pot-luck feast – this is simply a meal where everyone brings a plate of food to share.

❖ In circle, draw down the lunar energies by meditating with the beat of a single hoop drum. Then take it in turns to speak your intuitive insights. If you don't have a hoop drum, use any percussive instrument, such as clap sticks, castanets, or *ganza*: an egg-shaped hand percussion instrument similar to a maraca.

❖ Create a ritual – use the elements of sacred ceremony above as a template to affirm, charge, and amplify your New Moon intention using an incantation/chant.

❖ Read a women's wisdom story – such as a myth or a women's folktale like those found in the book *Women Who Run with the Wolves* by Clarissa Pinkola Estes – and discuss its themes and lessons.

SUMMARY

❖ Ritual is any act that helps us anchor change.

❖ Without constructive rituals, we create potentially harmful rituals in our search for meaning and belonging.

❖ Goddess-honoring folk gather to mark their life transitions and the highs and lows of the natural cycles.

❖ When raising and directing energy, be vigilant about observing the law of reciprocity.

Yin reflection time

Cast your mind back to how you've celebrated your life milestones to date. Which events were the most meaningful for you, and why? Now contemplate your next milestone. How has this chapter inspired you to mark it?

Chapter 11
Goddess symbolism

The sacred feminine path is that of the mystic – one who perceives life as *symbolic*. A mystic seeks to understand his or her experiences through accessing a framework of myths, symbols, and archetypes that map the inner terrain of the soul.

According to the Merriam-Webster dictionary, mysticism is: *The belief that spiritual truth, or ultimate reality, can be attained through subjective experience (such as intuition or insight).*[1] So as more people rediscover and practice the sacred feminine tradition of mysticism, it will become commonplace to hear them respond to certain situations by saying, 'That was symbolic': indicating they've just had an 'a-ha' moment.

For example, have you ever noticed that when you're really low on energy you then spot that your car is nearly out of fuel, or your laptop or phone is almost out of charge? That is *symbolic*, meaning your external reality is reflecting your inner state.

Why work with symbolism?

Everything in life is symbolic, so when we attune to this way of seeing our reality, moment-to-moment, we can interpret the symbols we notice around us as keys to access insight into our current life lesson. So if you want to accelerate your wisdom, simply pay more attention to symbols and equate yourself with their meaning. The more we familiarize ourselves with symbols, the less likely we are to repeat painful situations.

Having an awareness of the symbols we synchronistically encounter enables life to feel less of a struggle and more of a magical mystery tour, as we come to see how interconnected everything is. This reassures us that we're not alone and that the benevolent Universe, in all its guises, is our wise friend and teacher.

So while the Divine Source of life has both feminine and masculine expressions, the feminine perspective is one that takes into account our inner perceptions, reconnecting us with our soul. Only by integrating our outer experiences with our inner understanding do we become balanced. So if you wish to consciously heal and empower your feminine sense of Self, notice the signposts being offered from the Great Mother Goddess.

A guide to Goddess symbols and totems

The following are some of the most recognized symbols of the Goddess from around the world. Use the 'divination meaning' section for timely Goddess guidance – should one of these symbols cross your path. If the same symbol crosses your path three times, take this as a sign that you've passed an initiation to acquire a new level of understanding and empowerment. (Kind of like earning a new Girl Guide badge from the Goddess!)

Apple

Considered the 'fruit of the Goddess' as it contains the five-pointed star when cut diagonally, the apple was often gifted by the Goddess to questing heroes to assist their getting of wisdom. It's associated with the Isle of Avalon, or the Apple Isle, a mystery school that taught the traditions of the Goddess. The apple was once revered as the fruit sought from the Tree of Life.

Divination meaning: This is a call to initiation: to shift your perception of yourself and life through reawakening an appreciation of feminine qualities and the cyclic nature of life.

Bee

The priestesses who served in the Goddess temples of Aphrodite, the Goddess of Love, were called *melissae*, meaning 'bees.' In ancient Greece, honeycomb was considered sacred, on account of its hexagonal shape: the number six was associated with Aphrodite. Honey was used and revered as a preservative.[2]

Divination meaning: Rediscover the sweetness of life by reconnecting with the power of community. Work can be joyful when we share the load.

Chevron

 This is one of the earliest known Goddess symbols, along with the V and the zigzag. The chevron represents water, the feminine element whose presence ensured life and birds – winged ones who descended from the heights into the water. The chevron has been found on carved bones that date back to 30,000BCE. This symbol of feminine power was later appropriated as a symbol of military power, and a soldier who gained a higher rank was said to have 'earned his stripes.'[3]

Divination meaning: It's time to spread your wings and expand your sphere of influence after a time of deep descent. Reconnect with the big picture, like a bird.

Cow

 One of the oldest totems of the sacred feminine, cows were honored in ancient festivals because they sustained human life, ensuring our survival. Several creation myths attribute the milk of the Cow Goddess as the source of all life. The Cow Goddess was associated with the Moon and considered the Great Mother Goddess or Cosmic Mother. At Full Moon she was at her most luminous, and her feminine attributes were more accessible.

Divination meaning: Nurture yourself with human kindness in order to preserve and sustain your output. Live in alignment with the lunar phases (see Chapter 7) to better understand and manage your energy levels.

Grail cup

An ancient symbol of sacred feminine rituals, the Grail was the receptacle of the life-giving blood of the Goddess. Similarly, bowls, baskets, upward triangles, wells, and caves were synonymous with the sacred womb symbolized by the Grail cup.[4]

Divination meaning: Honor your menses as your sacred time to rest and replenish your energy. If you don't menstruate, take time out each New Moon to commune with your soul: spend time in solitude, doing whatever your intuition guides you to do.

Labyrinth

A labyrinth is similar to a maze, but it only has one entrance and exit, so it's considered a symbol of life and death. Oracle priestesses would use a finger to trace the shape of a hand-held labyrinth as a means of going 'within' for intuitive answers.

Divination meaning: This symbol is a calling card from the Crone Goddess, Hecate, who governs the crossroads of change. Call on her assistance to help you release what no longer serves you, by turning inward to connect with your deepest truth.

Owl

While birds are one of the oldest totems of the Goddess, the owl is one of the most revered for its association with the Crone, who embodies wisdom. This is due to owls' ability to see in the dark, and their piercing eyes, which look deep into our soul.

Divination meaning: The key to becoming wise lies in seeing and acknowledging our shadow thoughts and behaviors. Resist the urge to blame others and instead, examine the lesson you have manifested to learn, through your conscious or unconscious expectations or actions.

Pentagram

The five-pointed star is the shape the planet Venus makes as she moves through the cosmos. The pentagram symbol represents the five elements of creation: Air, Earth, Water, Fire and Spirit. Many people fear this sign, due to the smear campaign waged on sacred feminine symbols and customs that saw it inverted and appropriated as a sign of the Christian concept of the Devil.

Divination meaning: Venus is asking you to ensure you honor all the elements in your life by attending to your mind (Air), body (Earth), emotions (Water), energy (Fire), and soul (Spirit). This will help you to live in harmony with yourself and others.

Serpent

This is a symbol of healing and renewal in ancient Goddess-worshipping cultures, which performed sacred practices to awaken the serpent of kundalini (see Chapter 5). The serpent, like woman, renews through cyclic skin-shedding, and due to its contact with Mother Earth, was considered her messenger, so snakes assisted oracular priestesses with divination.

Divination meaning: It's time to ignite your passion for life through creative and expressive practices like ecstatic dance, chanting, and drumming. Through activating your inner fire, you'll find the courage to release whatever it is that's draining you.

Spider

In numerous indigenous creation myths, Great Grandmother Spider was said to 'weave the web of creation.' With her eight legs and figure-of-eight shape, she is a symbol of feminine power.

Divination meaning: Write down your ideas, or consider publishing poetry, prose, or a blog. Draw upon your community for support, knowing we are stronger when we weave our strengths together. It's time to own your personal power and create a new story.

Spiral

Appearing as far back as Paleolithic times, when it was carved on tombs, the spiral is a sacred feminine symbol of creation. It generates energy as a conductor of emanating life force. This is why spiral dances are used to raise group energy in sacred ceremonies. Participants hold hands in circle, and the ceremonial leader then lets go of one hand and begins leading everyone in a spiral toward the center of their sacred circle. Eventually, everyone is tightly wound as the energy winds to a climactic point to release the intent. Symbolic of the divine design of nature, the spiral signifies life eternal.[5]

Divination meaning: Trust that everything is unfolding exactly as it's meant to, even if it doesn't appear to be. If life doesn't make sense, spiral inward and center yourself at the epicenter of our spiraling galaxy. Alternatively, you're experiencing a growth spurt and this is a sign that it's safe to expand. It is a time of death and rebirth through a shift in perception.

The triple Moon

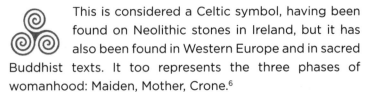 Also known as 'the triple-phase Goddess,' this symbol represents the three chronological phases of womanhood: Maiden, Mother, Crone. These are symbolized by the Waxing Crescent Moon, the Full Moon, and the Waning Crescent Moon.

Divination meaning: Attune to the lunar cycle to develop the gifts of each phase. This will help you to befriend your feminine sensitivities, rather than fearing or suppressing them.

Triskele (triple spiral)

This is considered a Celtic symbol, having been found on Neolithic stones in Ireland, but it has also been found in Western Europe and in sacred Buddhist texts. It too represents the three phases of womanhood: Maiden, Mother, Crone.[6]

Divination meaning: Seek to embody all three faces of the Goddess, regardless of your chronological age, and you'll not fear the cycles of time. Get to know the lessons and strengths of each Goddess phase (see Chapter 8).

Triquetra

 Known as the never-ending symbol, the ancient Celtic Triquetra is three interlocking gateways symbolizing the female vulva, which is the entrance to the Goddess and her mysteries. It's also found in Nordic inscriptions, on German coins, and on Swedish runes, and is associated with the union of the three realms: Earth, sea, and sky, and in more modern times, with mind, body, and Spirit.

Divination meaning: It's time to enter the mystery, so invoke the support of Sheela-na-Gig, the Crone Gatekeeper Goddess of the Mysteries, and walk in perfect love and perfect trust. Magic is afoot and an initiation is at hand!

How symbols strengthen our intuition

Intuition is simply our ability to access our inner guidance: that initial sense, knowing or feeling we receive when we meet someone for the first time, or when we enter a room. We access it by attuning our awareness to the information being relayed through our subtle senses, which are:

1. **Clairvoyance** (clear inner seeing)

2. **Clairsentience** (clear inner sensing)

3. **Clairaudience** (clear inner hearing)

4. **Precognition** (flashes of premonition)

5. **Intuition** (clear inner knowing).

Observing and interpreting symbols strengthens our intuition, as it hones our ability to read and navigate our external reality, connecting to our inner reality. Since our intuition is never wrong and relays feedback to us much faster than our rational analysis, this makes decision-making less stressful. Our intuition is the most reliable guidance system we have for avoiding potential danger.

The transformational power of symbols

Our subconscious mind only speaks in symbols, unlike our rational mind, which communicates through the language of words and numbers. Unsurprisingly, it's the subconscious part of our mind that drives 95 per cent of our external behaviors. The more we access what lies within our subconscious mind, the more whole and integrated our psyche.[7]

Practical ways to work with symbols

Symbols open the door to our subconscious, so we can retrieve soul memories from past incarnations, heal from trauma, anchor positive thought patterns, or enjoy more of those a-ha moments. Below are more ways to unlock the power of your mind's mainframe 'super-computer' – using the power of symbols.

Meditation

It's powerful to meditate on a symbol you feel drawn to. First, allow your eyes to focus on the center of the image, and then let them go out of focus. Allow your mind to wander, going deeper into the symbol as a portal to the inner worlds.

Alternatively, you may receive an image of a symbol in your mind's eye while doing a guided meditation. Always record any symbols you see, so you can look up their meaning to honor their message and integrate the lesson.

Dream analysis

Everything is symbolic in a dream, so keep a dream journal beside your bed to record your dream symbols. Over time, you may notice patterns with the symbols you receive at different times in your fertility cycle or the lunar cycle.

Sacred art

Drawing a symbol helps anchor its healing medicine and power within our energy field. So take note if you find yourself doodling an ancient symbol. Alternatively, consider joining a mandala art class to distill the power of one symbol at a time by drawing or painting it within a circle. This amplifies its energy within a vortex.

Magical sigils

A sigil is a symbol imbued with energetic intention, giving it magical power. It may be painted, drawn, or inscribed. You can create a personal sigil by combining those that speak strongly to your soul. Then use it as a signature, rubber stamp, or wax seal to sign letters, or use it as your business logo. Alternatively, you can condense the letters of your name into just a few strokes to form a sigil that distills your personal energetic signature.

Body art

Scarification and tattoos are permanent forms of body art used as initiations in indigenous cultures. They're becoming increasingly popular as people search for meaning through shamanic practices. Henna and red ochre are impermanent forms of body art that were sacred to Goddess traditions because they symbolized the sacred blood of our Moon cycle and its powerful magical properties. Wearing a symbol is an act of initiation that activates its lesson in our waking life.

Exercise: Goddess body art New Moon ritual

Use your intuition to select one of the symbols in the list above. Choose the one that draws you in, has the most energy, or speaks to you most strongly at this time. This will be the symbol that contains the healing medicine and power most relevant for your journey.

At the next New Moon, paint this symbol in henna on your feet and ask the Goddess to guide you in learning the lessons contained within it. Henna can be purchased at Asian grocers or online.

SUMMARY

✦ Mysticism is an experiential approach to spirituality; it is used in the Goddess tradition to navigate external experiences by attuning to our intuition.

✦ Observing symbols enables us to directly experience life as mystical through synchronistic symbolic interactions that directly relate to our life experiences. This experience tells us we are not alone, which decreases feelings of isolation and anxiety.

❖ Symbols help shed light on our current life lessons, so we can heal our unconscious patterns of thought and behavior.

❖ Our inner patterns of thought and behavior are reflected synchronistically in our external reality. So by identifying and interpreting the symbols we observe, we can heal our unconscious patterns.

❖ We can anchor the medicine of a symbol in our lives by wearing or drawing it.

Yin reflection time

Take a moment to gaze at the symbols featured in this chapter. You may wish to draw one repeatedly, allowing your mind to wander as you do so. Notice any sensations, images, feelings, or inspirational messages that surface.

Conclusion
Walking the Goddess path

It's one thing to acquire knowledge, but another to live it! So here are my suggestions for:

1. Embodying the sacred feminine through experiential practices.

2. Navigating your inevitable descent journeys to the Underworld.

3. Dealing with critics in a culture conditioned by patriarchal values.

Maintaining your Goddess frequency

Have you ever noticed that when you return from a holiday or a meditation retreat, your inner and outer glow fades as you go back to your mundane routines and responsibilities? So too, when we return from a descent journey to champion and integrate the lost parts of our sacred feminine identity, it can be a challenge to maintain our stature as a queen in our daily life.

'Before enlightenment, chopping wood, fetching water.
After enlightenment, chopping wood, fetching water.'
ZEN BUDDHIST PROVERB

So, how do we maintain our clarity, empowerment, and high energy levels as a vessel for the sacred feminine? By doing sacred practices on a regular, cyclic basis. For once we've unveiled our divine feminine nature, our life lessons continue. So it's essential that we support ourselves with sacred practices. Below are some suggestions:

The four paths of yoga

The four paths of yoga are ancient practices that developed in Indian settlements during the Neolithic period. They emerged from the Tantric and Vedic traditions that later combined to become the Hindu religion – a faith that honors both the sacred feminine and masculine.

Jnana yoga

When done regularly, Jnana yoga can align our outer and inner worlds. The practice includes physical postures, breath work, meditation, chants, symbols, hand positions, energy locks, and sacred sexual communion. You'll find all of these practices incorporated in kundalini yoga, whose sole focus is the activation and raising of Shakti. Jnana yoga is outlined in more detail in Chapter 5.

Bhakti yoga

Bhakti yoga is the path of devotional love. To activate our inner Goddess it's essential we open our devotional heart to the Cosmic Mother. This is done through our dedication to serve the divine as a vessel for divine will.

Since music is the fastest way to change our vibrational state (our energy level and mood), I recommend playing devotional music to the Goddess in your home and in your car. Just being in the frequency of those singing from an open devotional heart will elevate your consciousness and open your devotional heart, which reduces stress. My two favorite devotional music artists are Snatam Kaur and Jai-Jagdeesh.

I also recommend finding and attending a local Full Moon 'kirtan.' Kirtan is a devotional chanting practice that involves invoking the energies of the various God/Goddess aspects by singing their names in Sanskrit. When done with your eyes closed, and with a sincere intent of devotional communion, it's guaranteed to get you drunk on the bliss of an open devotional heart.

Karma yoga

Words are empty if they are not backed up by action. So this yogic path asks us to dedicate ourselves to acts of service that honor the lineage of the sacred teachings that have initiated us and alleviated our confusion and suffering.

In the Goddess tradition, this can include creating a Red Tent circle in your community, or ensuring the next generation of girls has access to their birthright of sacred feminine teachings and customs.

If you feel called to serve the Goddess, I recommend creating a self-styled ritual, using the elements of ceremony template in Chapter 10, to dedicate yourself as a clear channel to serve the Goddess, as this act unleashes our bounty of divine gifts.

I did this intuitively at the age of 26 by standing on my porch without any pomp or pageantry and saying out loud under the stars: 'I hereby dedicate myself to being a conduit for the Goddess in service as her priestess. From this day forth I will use only my priestess name, Tanishka.' As stated earlier, your own words, spoken from the heart with passion, are the most powerful.

Raja yoga

This yogic path develops our mind so we transcend petty thinking by dedicating ourselves to mental self-discipline. We do this through mindfulness, truthfulness, integrity, humility, and esoteric study. The key is to maintain self-enquiry in each moment, so our ego doesn't attach to false perceptions that create drama. Clear thinking leads to right action.[1]

Advice for living life large as a Goddess

I feel that, in addition to the sacred practices above, it's paramount to keep our cup of self-love full by making self-honoring choices. We can do this by spending regular time in nature and making time to enjoy moments of pleasure and beauty with those who share our values.

Find others walking the Goddess path

You may find it inspiring to attend a gathering with others who are reclaiming the ancient traditions of the sacred feminine. Try attending some of the Goddess festivals, temples, conferences, or Red Tents listed in the Resources section.

Take the spiral path of the Goddess

The Goddess path asks us to continually shed the old, and embrace the new – so we may fulfill our highest growth. That means surrendering and accepting the inevitable cyclic descents to the Underworld.

As you know now, the Underworld is the state within where no light dwells. It's the place where we meet our fears, self-doubt, and past wounds, which can feel overwhelming. The Goddess path provides a framework for navigating this terrain, so we can embrace the void of pure potential and rebirth ourselves with adequate support: in accordance with the natural cycles. If this path speaks to your soul, commit to finding a teacher who can act as a way-shower. Whether that's via books, online courses, retreats, or workshops, trust that if you seek, you will find, and you will know it when you find it.

Without a map, guidance or inspiration, many remain lost in the Underworld and are driven by their shadow self and unhealed wounds. They seek comfort through addictive substances, escape into virtual realities, or engage in destructive behaviors.

One doesn't need to look far to see the shadow cast upon the world due to the absence and distortion of the sacred feminine teachings and practices. There's a pandemic of souls trapped in the Underworld who are experiencing emotional and physical illness caused by a deeper soul sickness: the lack of integration between their inner and outer perceptions. The good news is that when things get this bad, people make it a priority to seek insight to pierce the darkness.

A guide to your descent journey

After reading about the descent journeys in Chapter 4, you may be wondering whether we endure more than one descent journey. The answer is yes: since life and learning are as eternal as the natural cycles that initiate us. The first descent journey is always the hardest because it's unfamiliar, and we haven't learned to trust the process.

This is why the first relationship break-up is the hardest, or the first time we birth a child, lose our job, relocate to another city, or experience the death of a close family member. The more resistance there is, the more suffering. And we resist when we lack adequate support.

The more we honor the cyclic nature of life, the easier it is to navigate the dark times. So do gift yourself the support of a teacher to assist you with your Moon rites, seasonal rites, and rites of passage, along with a circle of soul sisters who can act as spiritual midwives for your cyclic descents. There are books, websites, and online courses available that offer a range of perspectives on these ancient paths of initiation.

As always, use your intuition to discern what information resonates within you as truth, and exercise discernment when choosing a teacher. A great teacher will impart information and experiential processes in a way that feels empowering. So trust your feelings as your guide, and work with those who inspire your light to shine.

Dealing with critics

Given that we live in a culture that's been conditioned to mistrust, fear, and ridicule all that's held sacred by the feminine, you may encounter some opposition from those around you if you start espousing Goddess values. So how can you avoid being ostracized for your feminine perspective?

To avoid unnecessary conflict, use your intuition to assess the receptivity of the other person before sharing your feminine perspective. Not because you'll end up being burned at the stake or drowned in a river (fortunately, those days are behind us!), but because it's draining to share our enthusiasm with anyone who's closed and cynical. It's also pointless to try and educate those who aren't interested. Also keep in mind that imposing our views on another is disrespectful of their free will.

Embodiment is the path of least resistance

The most powerful thing we can do is 'walk the talk.' We need to live the Goddess principles by applying them in our own life, and eventually people will observe our grace, wisdom, and understanding, and seek us out when they're ready to hear our perspective.

Never forget that those who claim not to believe in anything esoteric, such as astrology, are still governed by the laws of nature, whether they believe in them or not. We are, after all, made up of oscillating particles of energy, so the cycles of the Sun, Moon, and seasons have an effect on our psyche – whether we stop to notice and make the connection or not. Fortunately, exoteric (physical) science is catching up with esoteric (metaphysical) science at a rapid rate.

Experience is the greatest teacher

'I never used to believe in any of this stuff' is a comment I often hear from those who follow my daily lunar guidance. Why is this? Learning is experiential. So those who start out skeptical cannot refute the evidence of how their daily experience matches the influences dictated by the natural cycles.

The Goddess path follows three sacred strands of learning:

1. **Knowledge**: what we learn from others, such as teachers, books, and courses.

2. **Wisdom**: what we learn from reflecting on our life experiences and lessons.

3. **Gnosis**: the voice of our inner knowing.

Stay curious and continue to quench your thirst for all three.

A final word

The peoples of the Old World in Europe who worshipped the Great Mother Goddess were referred to as the faery folk. They lived in barrows – mounds under hills – and interacted with the elemental beings: the nature spirits who share our home planet in the other dimensions.

These nature spirits were given colloquial names like 'Will-o'-the-wisp,' a reference to their astral bodies, which according to European folklore, glowed in woodlands at night.

Another term used was 'banshee,' a word derived from the Gaelic terms of both the Irish and Scottish, meaning 'woman of the faery mound.'

Known also as Tuatha De Danann or Aos Si, they were considered a supernatural race of beings once regarded as ancient Gods and Goddesses. In the 19th century, some archaeologists found underground rooms in Scotland's Orkney Islands resembling the Elfland described in the faerytale *Cuhilde Rowland*.

This prehistoric race of 'little people,' as they were also known, was said to have died out during the Iron Age, as human tribes became more hostile and the energetic frequency of our planet became more dense. They were the ones said to have built stone circles, and they knew how to live in harmony with all the worlds.

Their time was described as a golden age, just as our current Age of Aquarius was prophesied as an age of enlightenment when once more, the veils would lift and we would remember our multidimensional sensibilities and kin. We can see the herald of this return in the renewed interest in Middle Earth, magic, faeries, and dragons.

The birthing of this new era requires us all to make that descent journey to the womb of the Great Mother – in order to release our old way of being and seeing. With each person who willingly makes this return, we reawaken the Great Mother's age-old wisdom and grace, lighting the path for others to follow.

May we all heal our separation from the Great Mother, and in doing so, heal the wounded feminine in ourselves and in our world.

It has been my honor and pleasure to serve as your guide to the mysteries of the sacred feminine.

Blessings,

Tanishka

References

Chapter 1: The return of the sacred feminine

1. Merlin Stone, 1976: *When God Was A Woman*; USA: The Dial Press

2. Robert Ohotto, 2016: 'A Complete Tour of the Astrological Ages.' www.ohotto.com/features/astrological_ages_tour.asp (accessed 6 September, 2016)

3. Peter McBrearty, DMS Astrol: 'The Great Ages: The Age of Leo.' undersea.tripod.com/ageleo.htm (accessed 6 September, 2016)

4. Museum of Ancient and Modern Art. www.mama.org/exhibits/ancient/goddess/ (accessed 13 March, 2017)

5. en.wikipedia.org/wiki/Old_Europe_(archaeology) (accessed 13 March, 2017)

6. www.signsofthetimeshistory.com/ages.html (accessed 6 September, 2016)

7. www.crystalinks.com/enumaelish.html (accessed 13 March, 2017)

8. Sean Maddox, 2016: *When Time and Eternity Kiss*; Balboa Press, Bloomington, In 47403, USA

9. www.historyonthenet.com/mesopotamian-education-and-schools/ (accessed 13 March, 2017)

10. Laurence Gardner, 1999: *Genesis of the Grail Kings*; UK: Transworld Publishers

11. Jonathan Kirsch, 1997: *The Harlot By The Side of the Road: Forbidden Tales of the Bible*; New York: Ballantine Books, p.315.

12. Samuel Noah Kramer, 1962: 'The Biblical "Song of Songs" and the Sumerian Love Songs'. www.penn.museum/sites/expedition/the-biblical-song-of-songs-and-the-sumerian-love-songs/ (accessed 10 September, 2016)

13. Joshua J. Mark, 2009: 'Sargon of Akkad', Ancient History Encyclopedia. www.ancient.eu/Sargon_of_Akkad/ (accessed 18 October, 2016)

14. Jonathan Kirsch, 1997: *The Harlot By The Side of the Road: Forbidden Tales of the Bible*; New York: Ballantine Books, p.315.

15. Linda Lowen, 2009: 'The Dalai Lama – "The World Will Be Saved By the Western Woman." www.dharmacafe.com/index.php/news-briefs/article/the-dalai-lama-the-world-will-be-saved-by-the-western-woman (accessed 11 September, 2016)

16. James Plafke, 2013: 'Our Universe is a Hologram, and We're Floating Inside of It, Suggests New Research.' www.extremetech.com/extreme/172812-our-universe-is-a-hologram-and-were-floating-inside-of-it-suggests-new-research (accessed 11 September, 2016)

17. Ron Cowen, 2013: 'Simulations Back Up Theory That Universe is a Hologram.' www.nature.com/news/simulations-back-up-theory-that-universe-is-a-hologram-1.14328 (accessed 11 September, 2016)

18. Peter Dizikes, 2008: 'The Meaning of the Butterfly' archive.boston.com/bostonglobe/ideas/articles/2008/06/08/the_meaning_of_the_butterfly/ (accessed 11 September, 2016)

Chapter 2: Herstory: ancient Goddess cultures

1. Riane Eisler, 1987: *The Chalice and the Blade*; New York: Harper Collins

2. Monica Sjoo and Barbara Mor, 1987: *The Great Cosmic Mother*; New York: Harper and Row

3. Gerhard Bott 'Her Story' www.sacredfemalerising.com/en/about-us/her-story/ (accessed March 13, 2017)

4. Stephanie Pappas, 2016: 'Goddess Name Inscribed in Lost Language on Ancient Tablet.' www.livescience.com/55907-etruscan-tablet-holds-lost-language.html (accessed 21 August, 2016)

5. William Bond, 2006: 'Did Women Once Rule the World?' www.womanthouartgod.com/didwomanruletheworld.php (accessed 20 August, 2016)

6. Riane Eisler, 1987: *The Chalice and the Blade*; New York: Harper Collins

7. Vicki Noble, 1999: *Shakti Woman: Feeling Our Fire, Healing Our World*; New York: Harper Collins

8. Riane Eisler, 1987: *The Chalice and the Blade*; New York: Harper Collins

9. Barbara G. Walker, 1983: *The Woman's Encyclopedia of Myths & Secrets*; New York: Harper Collins

10. Merlin Stone, 1976: *When God Was A Woman*; USA: The Dial Press

11. Marija Gimbutas, 1989: *The Language of the Goddess*; New York: Thames and Hudson

12. 'Paleolithic Art in Japan': heritageofjapan.wordpress.com/pacing-the-paleolithic-path/paleolithic-art-in-japan/ (accessed 21 August, 2016)

13. Max Dashu, 2016: *Witches and Pagans: Women in European Folk Religion, 700–1100*; USA: Veleda Press

14. Marija Gimbutas, 1989: *The Language of the Goddess*; New York: Thames and Hudson

15. Serge Tigneres, SBS Australia 2006: 'Mesopotamia – The Sumerians.' www.youtube.com/watch?v=lESEb2-V1Sg (accessed 19 August, 2016)

16. Bruce Pascoe. Land Cultures: Aboriginal economies and permaculturefuturewww.youtube.com/watch?v=g2IrBoLbWU4&t=838s

17. Riane Eisler, 1987: *The Chalice and the Blade*; New York: Harper Collins

18. New World Encyclopedia, 2016: 'Matriarchy' www.newworldencyclopedia.org/entry/Matriarchy (accessed 22 August, 2016)

19. Wikipedia, 2016. en.wikipedia.org/wiki/Sargon_of_Akkad (accessed 22 August, 2016

20. Merlin Stone, 1976: *When God Was A Woman*; USA: The Dial Press

21. Riane Eisler, 1987: *The Chalice and the Blade*; New York: Harper Collins

22. Ibid

23. Riane Eisler, 1987: *The Chalice and the Blade*; New York: Harper Collins

Chapter 3: The Goddess tradition

1. Eloise Hart, 1985: 'The Delphic Oracle' www.theosophy-nw.org/theosnw/world/med/me-elo.htm (accessed 4 August, 2016)

2. Penelope Shuttle and Peter Redgrove, 1978: *The Wise Wound*; UK: Victor Gollancz Ltd

3. Barbara Ehrenreich, 1973: 'Witches, Midwives and Nurses.' www.marxists.org/subject/women/authors/ehrenreich-barbara/witches.htm (accessed 4 August, 2016)

4.   Ibid

5.   Barbara Ehrenreich, 1973: 'Witches, Midwives and Nurses.' www.marxists.org/subject/women/authors/ehrenreich-barbara/witches.htm (accessed 4 August, 2016)

Chapter 4: Core beliefs and the three pathways of initiation

1.   Vicki Noble, 1999: Shakti Woman: Feeling Our Fire, Healing Our World; New York: Harper Collins

2.   Cryo-cell International, Inc: 'Banking Menstrual Stem Cells.' www.cryo-cell.com/menstrual/stem-cells

3.   Jamie Sams, 1993: The 13 Clan Mothers; San Francisco: Harper SanFrancisco

Chapter 5: Shakti power

1.   Dr. Carmen Boulter, 2009: *The Pyramid Code*; Canada: Magdalena Productions

2.   Egyptian Mystery Schools www.unexplainedstuff.com/Religious-Phenomena/Egyptian-Mystery-Schools.html (accessed 13 March, 2017)

3.   James Dow Allen, 1998–2017 'The Greatest Mathematicians of the Past.' fabpedigree.com/james/mathmen.htm (accessed 13 March, 2017)

4.   George G. M. James, 1954: 'Stolen Legacy'; www.sacred-texts.com/afr/stle/stle05.htm (accessed March 13, 2017)

Chapter 6: The Wheel of Eight

1.   Babylon Sabbath of Marduk and Zarpanit – Shabbat, Shabatu. www.piney.com/BabFeastMard.html (accessed 13 March, 2017)

2.   Walter Warttig Mattfeld y de la Torrre, 2001. www.bibleorigins.net/ShabbatShapattu.html (accessed 25 August, 2016)

3.   Dr. Carmen Boulter, 2009: *The Pyramid Code*; Canada: Magdalena Productions

Chapter 7: Goddess phases of the lunar cycle

1.   Vicki Noble, 1999: Shakti Woman: Feeling Our Fire, Healing Our World; New York: Harper Collins

Chapter 8: Rites of passage

1. Susan Maushart, 1999: *The Mask of Motherhood*; USA: The New Books

2. Moe Bedard, 2015: 'Third Eye Blind: Calcification of the Hippocampus, Worms and Alzheimer's Disease.' gnosticwarrior. com/third-eye-blind.html (accessed 28 August, 2016)

3. Angelfire.com 'Hel, Norse Goddess of the Dead.' www.angelfire. com/journal/ofapoet/hel.html (accessed August 28, 2016)

4. Barbara G. Walker, 1988: *Women's Encyclopedia of Myths and Symbols*; New York: Harper Collins

5. Orel, Vladimir, 2003: *A Handbook of Germanic Etymology*; Boston: Brill pp.156,168.

Chapter 9: Secret women's business

1. Judy Grahn, 1993: Blood, Bread & Roses: How Menstruation Created the World; Boston: Beacon Press

2. Vicki Noble, 1999: Shakti Woman: Feeling Our Fire, Healing Our World; New York: Harper Collins

3. Dr. Mercola, 2013. 'Women Beware: Most Hygiene Products Contain Toxic Ingredients.' articles.mercola.com/sites/articles/ archive/2013/05/22/feminine-hygiene-products.aspx (accessed August 29, 2016)

4. Honey Colony, 2016: '4 Ways to Honor The Power of Menses.' www.honeycolony.com/article/the-power-of-menses/ (accessed 29 August, 2016)

5. Jamie Sams, 1990: Sacred Path Cards; New York: Harper SanFrancisco, pp.145–150

6. Brooke Medicine Eagle, 1991: Buffalo Woman Comes Singing New York; Ballantine Books p.339

Chapter 10: Goddess rituals and ceremonies

1. Josh Gwatkin: 'The ancient origins of the law of attraction.' www. unveilingknowledge.com/the-ancient-origins-of-the-law-of-attraction/ (accessed March 14, 2017)

2. Timothy Freke and Peter Gandy: *The Hermetica*; TarcherPerigee, 2008 (first published 1384)

3. en.wikipedia.org/wiki/History_of_Wicca (accessed March 14, 2017)

4. Judy Grahn, 1993: *Blood, Bread & Roses: How Menstruation Created the World*; Boston: Beacon Press

Chapter 11: Goddess symbolism

1. Noah Webster, 2003: *The Merriam-Webster Dictionary*; New York: Encyclopedia Britannica

2. Barbara Walker, 1988: *The Woman's Dictionary of Symbols and Sacred Objects*; New York: Harper Collins. pp. 42, 414, 472, 479

3. Marija Gimbutas, 1989: *The Language of the Goddess*; New York: Thames and Hudson

4. Barbara Walker, 1988: *The Woman's Dictionary of Symbols and Sacred Objects*; New York: Harper Collins.

5. Chitra Jha, 2012: 'Sacred Geometry.' www.lifepositive.com/sacred-geometry/ (accessed 30 August, 2016)

6. Exemplore.com; Claire, 2015: 'Pagan Symbols and Their Meanings.' exemplore.com/paganism/Pagan-Symbols-and-Their-Meanings (accessed 30 August, 2016)

7. Lifetrainings.com; Anando: 'Your Unconscious Mind Is Running Your Life.' www.lifetrainings.com/Your-unconscious-mind-is-running-you-life.html (accessed 30 August, 2016)

Conclusion: Walking the Goddess path

1. Ramesh Bjonnes, 2011: '3 Ways to View the Ancient History of Yoga.' www.elephantjournal.com/2011/08/3-ways-to-view-the-ancient-history-of-yoga/ (accessed October 31, 2016)

Resources

Ancient Goddess cultures

If you'd like to discover more about ancient Goddess cultures, here are a few suggestions for books and videos.

The Language of the Goddess, Marija Gimbutas (Thames and Hudson)

Shakti Woman: Feeling Our Fire, Healing Our World, Vicki Noble (Harper Collins)

The Chalice and the Blade, Riane Eisler (Harper Collins)

When God Was a Woman, Merlin Stone (Marboro Books)

Witches and Pagans: Women in European Folk Religion, 700–1100, Max Dashu (Veleda Press)

Goddess civilizations timeline: a video created by Constance Tippett: www.youtube.com/watch?v=thOgEh1xpjg

Goddess archetypes

Books

The Inner Goddess Makeover, Tanishka (Star of Ishtar Publishing)

Goddesses in Everywoman, Jean Shinoda Bolen (Harper Paperbacks)

The Goddess Within, Jennifer and Roger Woolger (Balantine Books)

Online course

The Inner Goddess Online Course, Tanishka
www.themoonwoman.com/inner-goddess-course

Kundalini raising

Books

The Inner Goddess Makeover and *Creating Sacred Union Within*, Tanishka (Star of Ishtar Publishing)

Yogini: Unfolding the Goddess Within, Shambhavi Chopra (Wisdom Tree)

Online course

The Inner Goddess Online Course, Tanishka
www.themoonwoman.com/inner-goddess-course

CDs/MP3s

Chakradance, Natalie Southgate; www.chakradance.com

Kundalini Dance, Leyolah Antara; www.kundalinidance.com/about-kd

The Inner Goddess Makeover/Chakra Workout, Tanishka; www.themoonwoman.com

Goddess sacred sites

Below are a handful of sacred sites sourced with the help of Karen Tate, who has collated an extensive list of them in her book *Sacred Places of Goddess: 108 Destinations* (Consortium of Collective Consciousness).

South Asia

Chausath Yogini Temple, Madhya Pradesh, India

Kumari Temple, Kathmandu, Nepal

Northern Europe

St. Brigid's Well, County Clare, Ireland

Newgrange, Boyne Valley, Ireland

Glastonbury Tor, Somerset, UK

Chartres Cathedral, Chartres, France

Southern Europe

Aphrodite Temple, Aphrodiasias, Turkey

Çatal Hüyük, near Konya, Turkey

Isis Temple, Delos, Greece

Middle East/Africa

Sekhmet Temple, Karnak, Egypt

Isis Temple, Philae, Egypt

Temple of Oshun, Osogbo, Nigeria

China

Pu Tuo Shan Sacred Island, Zhejiang province

South America

Sacred Waters of the Orisha, Bahai, Brazil

Basilica of our Lady of Aparecida, Aparecida, Brazil

Caribbean

Saut D'Eau waterfalls, Haiti

Goddess archaeological artifacts

To see artifacts preserved from the ancient Goddess-worshipping cultures, visit the following museums:

The Louvre, Paris, France

Pergamon Museum, Berlin, Germany

The British Museum, London, UK

The Museum of Anatolian Civilizations, Ankara, Turkey

Goddess temples, festivals, and Red Tents

Below is a list of Goddess temples currently operating, although this does not include the growing number of temples offering online services. Also included is a list of Goddess festivals and Red Tent directories, to enable you to find a public Red Tent women's circle.

Goddess temples

USA

The Goddess Temple of Ashland, Oregon
2253 Oregon Highway 99 (off W. Jackson Road)
Ashland, Oregon, 97520
www.goddesstempleashland.com

The Temple of Goddess Spirituality
PO Box 813, Indian Springs, Nevada, 89018
www.sekhmettemple.com

The Goddess Temple of Orange County
17905 Sky Park Circle, #A Irvine, California, 92614
www.goddesstempleoc.org/index.html

UK

Glastonbury Goddess Temple
Goddess House, Magdalene Street, Glastonbury, BA6 9EJ
www.goddesstemple.co.uk

Norfolk Goddess Temple
Norfolk, East Anglia
www.norfolkgoddesstemple.co.uk

Asia Pacific

Kalighat Kali Temple
Kolkuta, West Bengal, India
kalighattemple.com

Dakshineswar Kali Temple, India
Dakshineswar, India
www.dakshineswarkalitemple.org

Mahalakshmi Temple
Kolhapur, India
www.mahalaxmikolhapur.com

Pura Ulun Danu Batur, Bali
Jl. Kintamani, Batur Selatan, Kintamani, Kabupaten Bangli, Bali, Indonesia
www.bali.com/temple_Kintamani_Ulun-Danu-Batur_89.html

Goddess festivals and conferences

USA

Annual Women of Wisdom Conference
North Seattle College, 9600 College Way North, Seattle, Washington
www.womenofwisdom.org

AZ Goddess Conference
Peaceful Spirit Enrichment Center, N. 24th Ave, New River, Arizona
peacefulspiritcenter@gmail.com

Festival of the Goddess
near Dripping Springs, Texas
festivalofthegoddess.org/index.html

GoddessFest
Julia Davis Park Bandshell, Boise, Idaho
www.gtgatc.org

Goddess Festival
Santa Cruz Mountains, La Honda, California
goddess-festival.com

Goddess Spirit Rising (conference)
American Jewish University, Brandeis-Bardin Campus,
Simi Valley, California
goddessspiritrising.com

Herbal Conference
Black Mountain, North Carolina
www.sewisewomen.com

Pacific Women's Herbal Conference
Camp Hamilton, Monroe, Washington
www.pacificwomensherbalconference.com

Temple of Isis – Convocation
Isis Oasis Sanctuary, 20889 Geyserville Ave, Geyserville,
California, 95441
www.isisoasis.us/events

The Daughters of Diana Gathering
Angelus Oaks, California
www.daughtersofdianagathering.org

UK

Glastonbury Goddess Festival
Glastonbury, Somerset
www.goddessconference.com

Europe

Goddess Conference
Dolní Věstonice, Czech Republic
www.konferencebohyne.cz

Nordic Goddess Festival
Bankavägen 73, Fjärås, Hallands Län, Sweden
www.nordicgoddessfestival.com

Asia Pacific
Goddess Conference Australia
The Baden-Powell Scout Centre at Pennant Hills, New
South Wales, Australia
www.goddessconferenceaustralia.com/goddess

Red Tent directories

Global
www.redtentmovie.com/red_tents_near_you.html
www.themoonwoman.com/red-tent-directory
www.thedfapp.com

Europe
www.redtentdirectory.com

Asia Pacific
www.redtentaustralia.org/queensland

Red Tent App
thedfapp.com

Acknowledgements

I am grateful to Jen Powell, who opened my eyes to the Goddess, to the sisters at Hay House, UK, who entrusted me to write this book, and to my inner circle of women – Rochelle, Kelly, Deb, Christina, and Annie – who held my daughter so that publishing meeting could take place on the other side of the world.

Thanks to Tamara and Jen, for helping me with research and editing. Thanks to Pavlina, for her research on Goddess conferences, to Karen, for her assistance with sacred sites, and to Wendy, for offering me a haven to write – away from the chainsaws.

To Ariella, my daughter, for weathering my book-birthing process, along with my soul sisters Helen, Fyona, Naomi, Justine, Donalea, El, and Eliza, who midwifed me through the transition phase. Takes a village!

ABOUT THE AUTHOR

Tanishka is best known as 'The Moon Woman' and has over half a million followers of her daily blog offering intuitive guidance to live in tune with the lunar cycle. A bestselling author of five books, she has taught ancient feminine wisdom and practices for over 20 years. She is a leader in the global Red Tent movement, and has trained women in 43 countries to facilitate Red Tent women's circles.

A former stand-up comedienne and clairvoyant, Tanishka has captivated audiences around the world by decoding the greatest mystery of all time – the Holy Grail from the perspective of the sacred feminine. In 2015 she created The 28-day Happy Challenge, a not-for-profit project to raise funds, awareness, and support for women and children recovering from the trauma of human trafficking.

In addition to being a popular keynote speaker at conferences, summits, and festivals – both online and around the world – she writes for numerous magazines worldwide. Visit Tanishka's website to find out more about her online courses, books, CDs, and live events.

www.themoonwoman.com

HAY HOUSE

Look within

Join the conversation about latest products, events, exclusive offers and more.

f Hay House UK

🐦 @HayHouseUK

📷 @hayhouseuk

🖤 healyourlife.com

We'd love to hear from you!